ROWAN
MINI KNITS

15
Hand Knit Designs
For Children
Aged 3-12

quail studio

Credits

Photography
Quail Studio

Art Direction & Styling
Georgina Brant

Design Layout
Quail Studio

Models
Bianca & Henry

Our Knitters
Jane M, Fiona, Alison, Sarah C, Jane N, Amanda, Sarah M, Rebecca, Jackie, Ruth, Virag, Jane P, Sue, Ann, Delia, Marie, Katie, Morag, Emma, Vicky, Sarah N, Vivienne, Fiona R, Anita

First published in Great Britain in 2022 by
Quail Publishing Limited
Unit 15, Green Farm, Fritwell, Bicester, Oxfordshire,
OX27 7QU
E-mail: info@quailstudio.co.uk

Rowan Mini Knits
978-1-8384102-1-6

R O W A N
MINI KNITS

Rowan Mini Knits is a collection of 15 adorable Rowan designs, originally created for adults, but now scaled down in size to fit Children aged 3-12 years.

Create jumpers, hats and outfits that are not just practical but versatile. Designed to stand up to the rigours of play, yet delightful when it's time to shine.

Collection

Mini Plume
pattern pg 36

Mini Skibo
pattern pg 38

Mini Hepburn & Mini Tracy
pattern pg 40 & 43

Mini Bark
pattern pg 46

Mini Alexie
pattern pg 50

Mini Ellen
pattern pg 54

Mini Cornwallis
pattern pg 58

Mini Hank
pattern pg 60

Mini Barton
pattern pg 64

Mini Citron & Mini Pumpkin
pattern pg 68 & 70

Mini Bret
pattern pg 72

Mini Veronica
pattern pg 74

Mini Garrick
pattern pg 76

Mini Plume

by Martin Storey

pattern page 36

Mini Skibo

by Martin Storey

pattern page 38

10

Mini Hepburn & Mini Tracy

by ARNE & CARLOS

pattern page 40 & 43

Mini Bark

by Martin Storey

pattern page 46

Mini Alexie

by Martin Storey

pattern page 50

Mini Ellen

by Kaffe Fassett

pattern page 54

Mini Cornwallis

by Martin Storey

pattern page 58

Mini Hank

by Martin Storey

---

pattern page 60

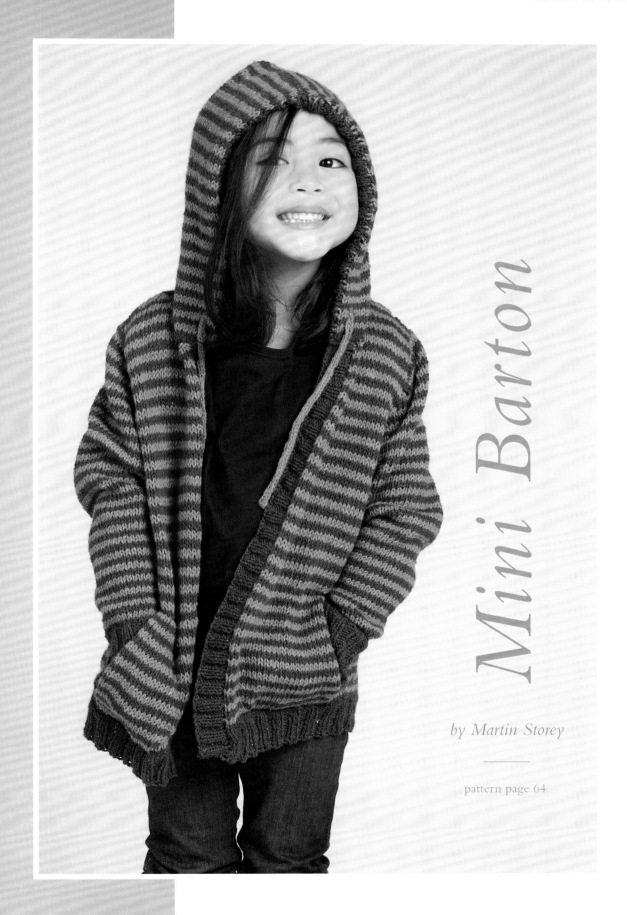

Mini Barton

by Martin Storey

pattern page 64

Mini Citron & Mini Pumpkin

by Quail Studio

pattern page 68 & 70

Mini Bret

by *Martin Storey*

pattern page 72

Mini Veronica

by Grace Jones

pattern page 74

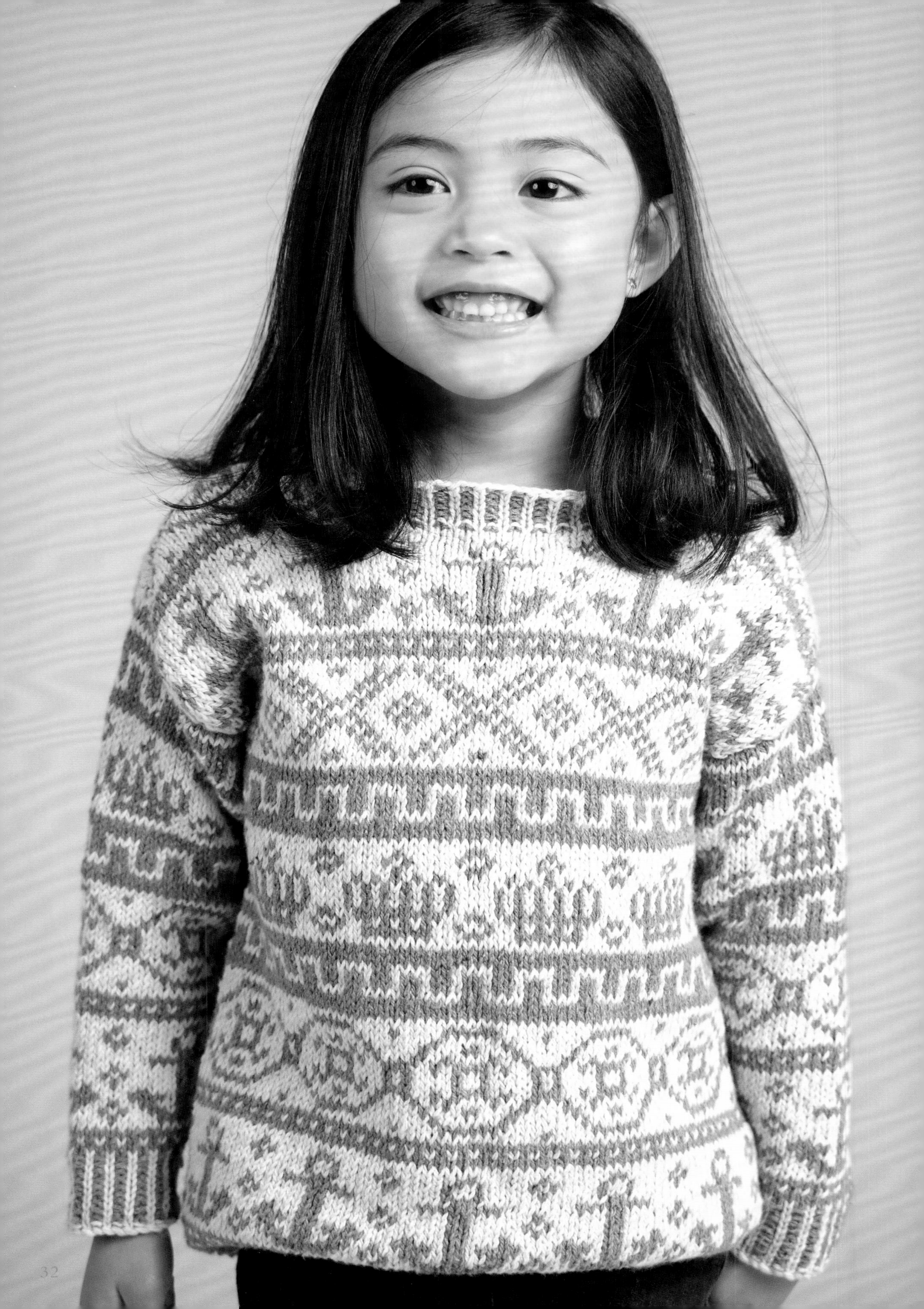

Mini Garrick

by Martin Storey

pattern page 76

Patterns

Mini Plume

by Martin Storey

● ● ●

image page 8

SIZE

To fit age

3-6	7-9	10-12	years

To fit chest

53-61	64-69	74-79	cm
21-24	25-27	29-31	in

Actual measurement of garment at lower edge

118	143	160	cm
46½	56¼	63	in

YARN

Alpaca Soft DK

A Charcoal 211

2	3	3	x 50gm

B Rainy Day 210

1	2	2	x 50gm

NEEDLES

4 double-pointed 3¼mm (no 10) (US 3) needles
4 double-pointed 4mm (no 8) (US 6) needles

Note: If preferred, garment can be knitted on circular needles but needles of differing lengths will be required.

TENSION

22 sts and 30 rows to 10 cm measured over plain st st, 25 sts and 26 rows to 10 cm measured over patterned st st, both using 4mm (US 6) needles.

PONCHO (Knitted in one piece, beg at hem edge)
Using double-pointed 3¼mm (US 3) needles and yarn A cast on 312 [376: 420] sts.
Distribute sts evenly over 3 of the 4 needles and, using 4th needle and taking care not to twist cast-on edge, work in rounds as folls:
Round 1 (RS): *K2, P2, rep from * to end.
This round forms rib.
Work in rib for a further 5 [5: 6] rounds.
Next round: Rib 2 [7: 8], work 2 tog, (rib 4, work 2 tog) 51 [60: 67] times, rib 2 [7: 8]. 260 [315: 352] sts.
Change to double-pointed 4mm (US 6) needles.
Next round (RS): Knit.
This round forms st st (K every round).
Work 2 [0: 1] more rounds.
10-12 years only
Next round: (K2tog, K20) − [-: 16] times. 336 sts.
Work 7 rounds.
7-9 and 10-12 years only
Next round: (K19, K2tog) − [15: 16] times. − [300: 320] sts.
All sizes
Work 0 [11: 11] rounds.
Next round: (K2tog, K18) 13 [15: 16] times. 247 [285: 304] sts.
Work 9 rounds.
Next round: (K17, K2tog) 13 [15: 16] times. 234 [270: 288] sts.
Work 1 round.
Place chart
Join in yarn B.
Beg and ending rounds as indicated, using the **fairisle** technique as described on the information page and repeating the 18-st patt repeat 13 [15: 16] times around each round, cont in patt from chart, which is worked entirely in st st, as folls:
Work 12 rounds.
Round 13: (K2tog, K16) 13 [15: 16] times. 221 [255: 272] sts.
Work 5 rounds.
Round 19: (K15, K2tog) 13 [15: 16] times. 208 [240: 256] sts.
Work 3 rounds.

Round 23: (K2tog, K14) 13 [15: 16] times. 195 [225: 240] sts.
Work 5 rounds.
Round 29: (K13, K2tog) 13 [15: 16] times. 182 [210: 224] sts.
Work 3 rounds.
Round 33: (K2tog, K12) 13 [15: 16] times. 169 [195: 208] sts.
Work 5 rounds.
Round 39: (K11, K2tog) 13 [15: 16] times. 156 [180: 192] sts.
Work 3 rounds.
Round 43: (K2tog, K10) 13 [15: 16] times. 143 [165: 176] sts.
Work 3 rounds.
Round 47: (K9, K2tog) 13 [15: 16] times. 130 [150: 160] sts.
Work 1 round.
Round 49: (K2tog, K8) 13 [15: 16] times. 117 [135: 144] sts.
Work 1 round.
Round 51: (K7, K2tog) 13 [15: 16] times. 104 [120: 128] sts.
Work 5 rounds.
Round 57: (K2tog, K6) 13 [15: 16] times. 91 [105: 112] sts.
Work 5 rounds, ending after round 62.
Break off yarn B and cont using yarn A only.
Work 1 round, inc [dec: -] 1 [1: -] st at end of round.
92 [104: 112] sts.
Work neckband
Change to double-pointed 3¼mm (US 3) needles.
Work in rib as given for cast-on edge for 6 [7: 8] rounds.
Cast off **loosely** in rib. (**Note**: Make sure cast-off edge will
stretch sufficiently to easily fit over child's head!).

MAKING UP
Press as described on the information page.
See information page for finishing instructions.

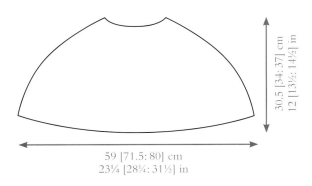

30.5 [34: 37] cm
12 [13½: 14½] in

59 [71.5: 80] cm
23¼ [28¼: 31½] in

Plume Chart

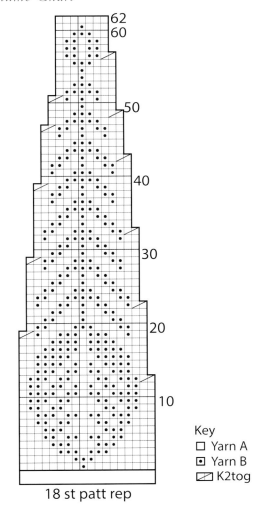

62
60

50

40

30

20

10

Key
☐ Yarn A
⊡ Yarn B
⧄ K2tog

18 st patt rep

Mini Skibo

by Martin Storey

● ● ●

image page 10

―――――――

SIZE

To fit age

3-6	7-9	10-12	years

To fit chest

53-61	64-69	74-79	cm
21-24	25-27	29-31	in

Actual measurement of garment at lower edge

120	140	160	cm
47¼	55	63	in

YARN

Alpaca Classic

4	5	6	x 25gm

(photographed in Feather Grey Melange 101)

NEEDLES

4 double-pointed 3¼mm (no 10) (US 3) needles
4 double-pointed 3¾mm (no 9) (US 5) needles
Cable needle

Note: If preferred, garment can be knitted on circular needles but needles of differing length will be required.

TENSION

22 sts and 28 rows to 10 cm measured over moss st using 3¾mm (US 5) needles. Cable panel (45 sts) measures 16 cm.

SPECIAL ABBREVIATIONS

Cr3L = slip next 2 sts onto cable needle and leave at front of work, P1, then K2 from cable needle; **Cr3R** = slip next st onto cable needle and leave at back of work, K2, then P1 from cable needle; **MB** = make bobble as folls: (K1, yfwd, K1) all into next st, turn, P3, turn, K3, turn, P3, turn, sl 1, K2tog, psso – bobble completed; **Tw5R** = slip next 3 sts onto cable needle and leave at back of work, K2, slip centre st of this group of 5 sts back onto left needle and P this st, then K2 from cable needle.

PONCHO (Knitted in one piece, beg at neck edge)
Using double-pointed 3¼mm (US 3) needles cast on 96 [104: 112] sts. (**Note**: Ensure this cast-on edge is worked loosely enough to fit over child's head!)
Distribute sts evenly over 3 of the 4 needles and, using 4th needle and taking care not to twist cast-on edge, work in rounds as folls:
Round 1 (RS): ★K2, P2, rep from ★ to end.
This round forms rib.
Work in rib for a further 23 [25: 27] rounds.
Next round: ★Rib 10, M1, (rib 11, M1) twice, rib 13 [15: 17], M1, rib 3 [5: 7], rep from ★ once more. 104 [112: 120] sts.
This completes neckband section.
Now work main body section as folls:
Change to double-pointed 3¾mm (US 5) needles.
Round 1 (RS): ★Place marker on needle, work 45 sts as row 1 of chart, place marker on needle, K1, (P1, K1) 3 [5: 7] times, rep from ★ once more. 108 [116: 124] sts.
Round 2: ★Slip marker onto right needle, work next 45 sts as row 2 of chart, slip marker onto right needle, M1, P1, (K1, P1) 3 [5: 7] times, M1, rep from ★ once more. 108 [116: 124] sts.
These 2 rounds set the sts – 2 cable panels with moss st either side.
Repeating the 20-row cable panel patt rep throughout and keeping moss st correct as now set, taking all inc sts into moss st, cont as folls:
Round 3: (Slip marker onto right needle, patt 45 sts, slip marker onto right needle, M1, moss st to next marker, M1) twice.
Rep last round 19 [23: 27] times more. 188 [212: 236] sts.
Next round: (Slip marker onto right needle, patt 45 sts, slip marker onto right needle, moss st to next marker) twice.
Next round: (Slip marker onto right needle, patt 45 sts, slip marker onto right needle, M1, moss st to next marker, M1) twice.
Rep last 2 rounds 10 [15: 22] times more. 232 [276: 328] sts.
Keeping sts correct as now set, cont as folls:
Work 3 rounds.

Next round: (Slip marker onto right needle, patt 45 sts, slip marker onto right needle, M1, moss st to next marker, M1) twice.
Rep last 4 rounds 12 [12: 10] times more. 284 [328: 372] sts.
Work 4 rounds.
Change to double-pointed 3¼mm (US 3) needles.
Work in rib as given for neckband section for 8 [9: 10] rounds.
Cast off **loosely** in rib.

MAKING UP
Press as described on the information page.
See information page for finishing instructions.

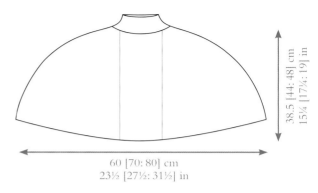

38.5 [44: 48] cm
15¼ [17¼: 19] in

60 [70: 80] cm
23½ [27½: 31½] in

Skibo Chart

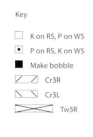

Key

- ☐ K on RS, P on WS
- ▣ P on RS, K on WS
- ■ Make bobble
- ⤬ Cr3R
- ⤬ Cr3L
- ⤬ Tw5R

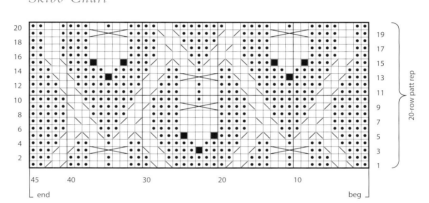

20-row patt rep

Mini Hepburn

by ARNE & CARLOS

image page 12

SIZE

To fit age

| 3-4 | 5-6 | 7-8 | 9-10 | 11-12 | years |

To fit chest

| 53-56 | 59-61 | 64-66 | 69-74 | 76-79 | cm |
| 21-22 | 23-24 | 25-26 | 27-29 | 30-31 | in |

Actual chest measurement of garment

| 70 | 76.5 | 81 | 88 | 94.5 | cm |
| 27½ | 30 | 32 | 34¾ | 37¼ | in |

YARN

Cotton Cashmere

A Linen 211

| 3 | 3 | 4 | 4 | 4 | x 50gm |

B Coral Spice 214

| 1 | 1 | 1 | 1 | 2 | x 50gm |

NEEDLES

1 pair 3¼mm (no 10) (US 3) needles
1 pair 4mm (no 8) (US 6) needles

TENSION

18 sts and 27 rows to 10 cm measured over patt using 4mm (US 6) needles.

Pattern note: When working patt from chart, take care to ensure each dec of patt is matched by an inc. If there are insufficient sts to work both, work end sts of rows in st st.

BACK

Using 3¼mm (US 3) needles and yarn B cast on 62 [70: 74: 78: 86] sts.

Row 1 (RS): K2, *P2, K2, rep from * to end.

Row 2: P2, *K2, P2, rep from * to end.

These 2 rows form rib.

Cont in rib for a further 8 [8: 10: 10: 10] rows, inc [dec: dec: inc: dec] 1 st at end of last row and ending with RS facing for next row. 63 [69: 73: 79: 85] sts.

Break off yarn B and join in yarn A.

Change to 4mm (US 6) needles.

Beg and ending rows as indicated and repeating the 20-row patt repeat throughout, cont in patt from chart as folls:

Cont straight until back meas 31.5 [34.5: 37.5: 40.5: 42.5] cm, ending with RS facing for next row.

Shape shoulders and back neck

Next row (RS): Cast off 6 [7: 7: 8: 9] sts, patt until there are 16 [17: 18: 19: 20] sts on right needle and turn, leaving rem sts on a holder.

Work each side of neck separately.

Keeping patt correct, dec 1 st at neck edge of next 3 rows, ending with RS facing for next row, **and at same time** cast off 6 [7: 7: 8: 9] sts at beg of 2nd row.

Cast off rem 7 [7: 8: 8: 8] sts.

Return to sts left on holder and slip centre 19 [21: 23: 25: 27] sts onto another holder (for neckband). Rejoin yarn with RS facing and patt to end. Complete to match first side, reversing shapings.

LEFT FRONT

Using 3¼mm (US 3) needles and yarn B cast on 31 [35: 35: 39: 43] sts.

Row 1 (RS): *K2, P2, rep from * to last 3 sts, K3.

Row 2: K1, P2, *K2, P2, rep from * to end.

These 2 rows form rib.

Cont in rib for a further 8 [8: 10: 10: 10] rows, – [dec: inc: –: dec] – [1: 1: –: 1] st at end of last row and ending with RS facing for next row. 31 [34: 36: 39: 42] sts.

Break off yarn B and join in yarn A.

Change to 4mm (US 6) needles.

Beg and ending rows as indicated, cont in patt from chart as folls:

Cont straight until 10 [12: 12: 12: 14] rows less have been worked than on back to beg of shoulder shaping, ending with RS facing for next row.

Shape front neck

Next row (RS): Patt 25 [28: 29: 31: 34] sts and turn, leaving rem 6 [6: 7: 8: 8] sts on a holder (for neckband).

Keeping patt correct, dec 1 st at neck edge of next 4 rows, then on foll 2 [3: 3: 3: 4] alt rows. 19 [21: 22: 24: 26] sts.

Work 1 row, ending with RS facing for next row.

Shape shoulder

Cast off 6 [7: 7: 8: 9] sts at beg of next and foll alt row.

Work 1 row.

Cast off rem 7 [7: 8: 8: 8] sts.

RIGHT FRONT

Using 3¼mm (US 3) needles and yarn B cast on 31 [35: 35: 39: 43] sts.

Row 1 (RS): K3, *P2, K2, rep from * to end.

Row 2: P2, *K2, P2, rep from * to last st, K1.

These 2 rows form rib.

Cont in rib for a further 8 [8: 10: 10: 10] rows, – [dec: inc: –: dec] – [1: 1: –: 1] st at end of last row and ending with RS facing for next row. 31 [34: 36: 39: 42] sts.

Break off yarn B and join in yarn A.

Change to 4mm (US 6) needles.

Beg and ending rows as indicated, cont in patt from chart as folls:

Cont straight until 10 [12: 12: 12: 14] rows less have been worked than on back to beg of shoulder shaping, ending with RS facing for next row.

Shape front neck

Next row (RS): Using yarn B, K6 [6: 7: 8: 8] and slip these sts onto a holder (for neckband – set this ball of yarn B aside with these sts), using yarn A patt to end. 25 [28: 29: 31: 34] sts.

Complete to match left front, reversing shapings.

SLEEVES

Using 3¼mm (US 3) needles and yarn B cast on 26 [26: 26: 30: 30] sts.

Work in rib as given for back for 10 [10: 12: 12: 12] rows, dec [inc: inc: dec: dec] 1 st at end of last row and ending with RS facing for next row. 25 [27: 27: 29: 29] sts.

Break off yarn B and join in yarn A.

Change to 4mm (US 6) needles.

Beg and ending rows as indicated, cont in patt from chart as folls:

Inc 1 st at each end of 5th [5th: 5th: 5th: 3rd] and every foll 6th row until there are 29 [37: 51: 51: 61] sts, then on 5 [4: 0: 2: 0] foll 8th rows, taking inc sts into patt. 39 [45: 51: 55: 61] sts.

Note: Sleeve shaping is only shown on chart for first 20-row patt repeat. Cont straight until sleeve meas 26 [30: 35: 39: 44] cm, ending with RS facing for next row.

Shape top

Cast off 6 [7: 8: 9: 10] sts at beg of next 2 rows, then 7 [8: 9: 9: 10] sts at beg of foll 2 rows.

Cast off rem 13 [15: 17: 19: 21] sts.

MAKING UP

Press as described on the information page.

Join both shoulder seams.

Neckband

With RS facing, using 3¼mm (US 3) needles and ball of yarn B set aside with right front, slip 6 [6: 7: 8: 8] sts on right front holder onto right needle, using ball of yarn B already attached, pick up and knit 13 [16: 16: 16: 17] sts up right side of front neck, and 3 sts down right side of back neck, K across 19 [21: 23: 25: 27] sts on back holder inc 1 st at centre, pick up and knit 3 sts up left side of back neck, and 13 [16: 16: 16: 17] sts down left side of front neck, then K across 6 [6: 7: 8: 8] sts on left front holder. 64 [72: 76: 80: 84] sts.

Row 1 (WS): K1, P2, *K2, P2, rep from * to last st, K1.

Row 2: K3, *P2, K2, rep from * to last st, K1.

These 2 rows form rib.

Work in rib for a further 5 [5: 7: 7: 7] rows, ending with RS facing for next row.

Cast off in rib.

Button band

With RS facing, using 3¼mm (US 3) needles and yarn B, pick up and knit 60 [64: 72: 76: 80] sts evenly down entire left front opening edge, from top of neckband to cast-on edge.

Beg with row 1, work in rib as given for neckband for 7 rows, ending with RS facing for next row.

Cast off in rib.

Work other side to match.

Mark points along side seam edges 12 [13.5: 15: 16.5: 18] cm either side of shoulder seams (to denote base of armhole openings). See information page for finishing instructions, setting in sleeves using the straight cast-off method.

Join side and sleeve seams.

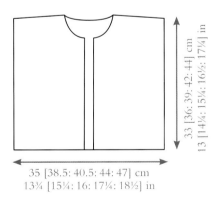

35 [38.5: 40.5: 44: 47] cm
13¾ [15¼: 16: 17¼: 18½] in

33 [36: 39: 42: 44] cm
13 [14¼: 15¼: 16½: 17¼] in

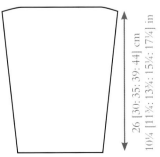

26 [30: 35: 39: 44] cm
10¼ [11¾: 13¾: 15¼: 17¼] in

Hepburn Chart

Key

- K on RS, P on WS
- yfwd
- K2tog
- sl 1, K1, psso
- sl1, K2tog, psso

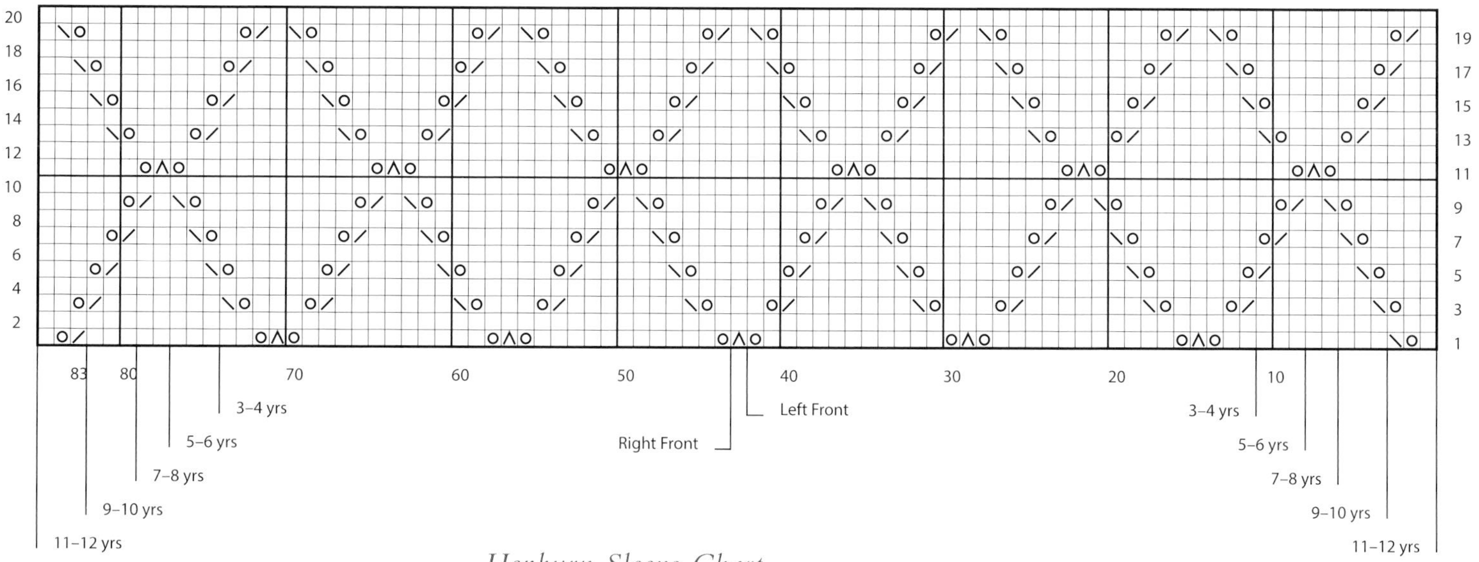

Hepburn Sleeve Chart

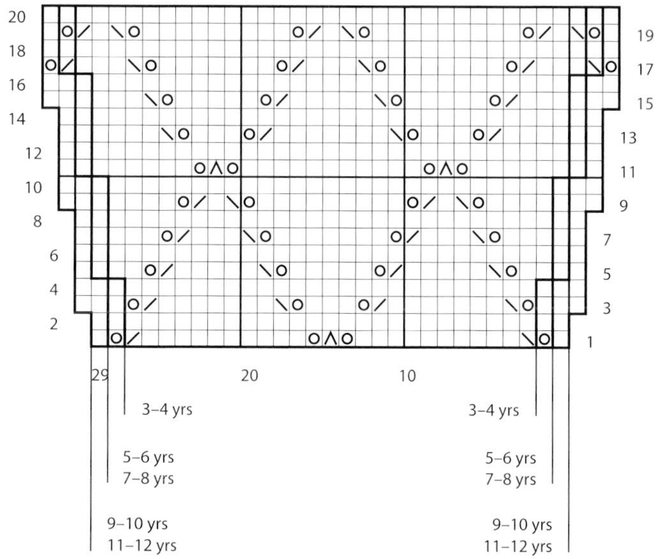

Key

- K on RS, P on WS
- yfwd
- K2tog
- sl 1, K1, psso
- sl1, K2tog, psso

Mini Tracy

by ARNE & CARLOS

image page 12

_____

SIZE

To fit age

3-4	5-6	7-8	9-10	11-12	years

To fit chest

53-56	59-61	64-66	69-74	76-79	cm
21-22	23-24	25-26	27-29	30-31	in

Actual chest measurement of garment

61	65.5	70	76.5	81	cm
24	25¾	27½	30	32	in

YARN

Cotton Cashmere

A Linen 211

2	2	2	3	3	x 50gm

B Coral Spice 214

1	1	1	1	1	x 50gm

NEEDLES

1 pair 3¼mm (no 10) (US 3) needles
1 pair 4mm (no 8) (US 6) needles

TENSION

18 sts and 27 rows to 10 cm measured over patt using 4mm (US 6) needles.

Pattern note: When working patt from chart, take care to ensure each dec of patt is matched by an inc. If there are insufficient sts to work both, work end sts of rows in st st.

BACK

Using 3¼mm (US 3) needles and yarn B cast on 54 [58: 62: 70: 74] sts.
Row 1 (RS): K2, ★P2, K2, rep from ★ to end.
Row 2: P2, ★K2, P2, rep from ★ to end.
These 2 rows form rib.
Cont in rib for a further 8 [8: 10: 10: 10] rows, inc [inc: inc: dec: dec] 1 st at end of last row and ending with RS facing for next row. 55 [59: 63: 69: 73] sts.
Break off yarn B and join in yarn A.
Change to 4mm (US 6) needles.
Beg and ending rows as indicated and repeating the 20-row patt repeat throughout, cont in patt from chart as foll s:
Cont straight until back meas 22.5 [24: 26.5: 28: 29.5] cm, ending with RS facing for next row.
Shape armholes
Keeping patt correct, cast off 3 [3: 3: 4: 4] sts at beg of next 2 rows. 49 [53: 57: 61: 65] sts.
Dec 1 st at each end of next 3 rows, then on foll 2 [3: 4: 4: 4] alt rows. 39 [41: 43: 47: 51] sts.
Cont straight until armhole meas 12 [13.5: 15: 16.5: 18] cm, ending with RS facing for next row.
Shape shoulders and back neck
Next row (RS): Cast off 3 sts, patt until there are 8 [8: 8: 9: 10] sts on right needle and turn, leaving rem sts on a holder.
Work each side of neck separately.
Keeping patt correct, dec 1 st at neck edge of next 3 rows, ending with RS facing for next row, **and at same time** cast off 3 sts at beg of 2nd row.
Cast off rem 2 [2: 2: 3: 4] sts.
Return to sts left on holder and slip centre 17 [19: 21: 23: 25] sts onto another holder (for neckband). Rejoin yarn with RS facing and patt to end. Complete to match first side, reversing shapings.

FRONT

Work as given for back until 14 [16: 16: 16: 18] rows less have been worked than on back to beg of shoulder shaping, ending with RS facing for next row.

Shape front neck

Next row (RS): Patt 15 [16: 16: 17: 19] sts and turn, leaving rem sts on a holder.

Work each side of neck separately.

Keeping patt correct, dec 1 st at neck edge of next 4 rows, then on foll 2 [3: 3: 3: 4] alt rows, then on foll 4th row. 8 [8: 8: 9: 10] sts.

Work 1 row, ending with RS facing for next row.

Shape shoulder

Cast off 3 sts at beg of next and foll alt row.

Work 1 row.

Cast off rem 2 [2: 2: 3: 4] sts.

Return to sts left on holder and slip centre 9 [9: 11: 13: 13] sts onto another holder (for neckband). Rejoin yarn with RS facing and patt to end. Complete to match first side, reversing shapings.

MAKING UP

Press as described on the information page.

Join right shoulder seam.

Neckband

With RS facing, using 3¼mm (US 3) needles and yarn B, pick up and knit 15 [16: 16: 16: 19] sts down left side of front neck, K across 9 [9: 11: 13: 13] sts on front holder, pick up and knit 15 [16: 16: 16: 19] sts up right side of front neck, and 3 sts down right side of back neck, K across 17 [19: 21: 23: 25] sts on back holder, then pick up and knit 3 sts up left side of back neck. 62 [66: 70: 74: 82] sts.

Beg with row 2, work in rib as given for back for 4 [4: 6: 6: 6] rows, ending with **WS** facing for next row.

Cast off **loosely** in rib with bigger needle (on **WS**). (**Note:** Make sure cast-off edge will stretch sufficiently to easily fit over child's head!)

Join left shoulder and neckband seam.

Armhole borders (both alike)

With RS facing, using 3¼mm (US 3) needles and yarn B, pick up and knit 50 [54: 62: 70: 74] sts evenly all round armhole edge.

Beg with row 2, work in rib as given for back for 4 [4: 6: 6: 6] rows, ending with **WS** facing for next row.

Cast off in rib (on **WS**).

Join side and armhole border seams.

See information page for finishing instructions.

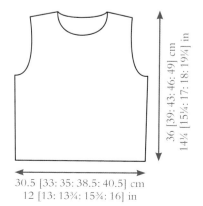

36 [39: 43: 46: 49] cm
14¼ [15¼: 17: 18: 19¼] in

30.5 [33: 35: 38.5: 40.5] cm
12 [13: 13¾: 15¾: 16] in

Tracy Chart

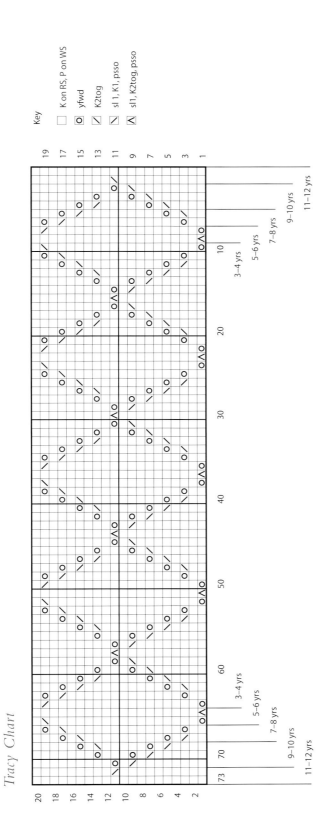

Key

☐	K on RS, P on WS
O	yfwd
╱	K2tog
╲	sl 1, K1, psso
⋀	sl1, K2tog, psso

Mini Bark

by Martin Storey

● ● ●

image page 14

SIZE

To fit age

3-4	5-6	7-8	9-10	11-12	years

To fit chest

53-56	59-61	64-66	69-74	76-79	cm
21-22	23-24	25-26	27-29	30-31	in

Actual chest measurement of garment

62.5	68	72	77.5	84.5	cm
24½	26¾	28¼	30½	33¼	in

YARN

Softyak DK
Sweater
A Cream 230

4	4	5	5	6	x 50gm

B Black 250

1	1	1	1	1	x 50gm

Dress

4	4	5	6	7	x 50gm

(photographed in Steppe 231)

Note: For dress, ignore instructions to change yarn colour and work motif using Purl sts on RS and Knit sts on WS rows. For sweater, work motif in st st and follow colours.

NEEDLES

1 pair 3¼mm (no 10) (US 3) needles
1 pair 4mm (no 8) (US 6) needles
Set of 4 double-pointed 3¼mm (no 10) (US 3) needles

TENSION

22 sts and 30 rows to 10 cm measured over st st using 4mm (US 6) needles.

BACK

Using 3¼mm (US 3) needles and yarn B cast on 78 [86: 90: 98: 106] sts.
Row 1 (RS): K2, *P2, K2, rep from * to end.
Row 2: P2, *K2, P2, rep from * to end.
These 2 rows form rib.
Break off yarn B and join in yarn A.
Cont in rib until back meas 6 [6: 6: 7: 7] cm, ending with **WS** facing for next row.
Next row (WS): Rib 2 [2: 4: 6: 4], work 2 tog, (rib 7 [6: 6: 5: 6], work 2 tog) 8 [10: 10: 12: 12] times, rib 2 [2: 4: 6: 4]. 69 [75: 79: 85: 93] sts.
Change to 4mm (US 6) needles.
Beg with a K row, now work in st st throughout as folls:
Sweater version only
Cont straight until back meas 27 [29.5: 31.5: 33.5: 35] cm, ending with RS facing for next row.
Dress version only
Cont straight until back meas 34 [34.5: 41: 45.5: 46] cm, ending with RS facing for next row.
Both versions
Shape raglan armholes
Cast off 3 sts at beg of next 2 rows. 63 [69: 73: 79: 87] sts.
Next row (RS): K2, K2tog, K to last 4 sts, K2tog tbl, K2.
Working all raglan armhole decreases as set by last row, dec 1 st at each end of 2nd [2nd: 4th: 4th: 4th] and 0 [0: 1: 1: 0] foll 4th row, then on foll 15 [17: 17: 19: 23] alt rows. 29 [31: 33: 35: 37] sts.
Work 1 row, ending with RS facing for next row.
Break yarn and leave sts on a holder.

FRONT

Work as given for back sweater and dress until 42 [40: 38: 36: 34] rows less have been worked than on back to beg of raglan armhole shaping, ending with RS facing for next row.

Place motif

Next row (RS): Using yarn A K11 [14: 16: 19: 23], work next 47 sts as row 1 of motif chart, using yarn A K11 [14: 16: 19: 23].

Next row: Using yarn A P11 [14: 16: 19: 23], work next 47 sts as row 2 of motif chart, using yarn A P11 [14: 16: 19: 23]. These 2 rows set the sts – central 47 sts worked from motif chart and sts either side in st st using yarn A.

Keeping sts correct as set and working appropriate rows of chart, work 40 [38: 36: 34: 32] more rows.

Shape raglan armholes

Keeping patt correct, cast off 3 sts at beg of next 2 rows. 63 [69: 73: 79: 87] sts.

Working all raglan armhole decreases as given for back, dec 1 st at each end of next and 0 [0: 2: 2: 1] foll 4th rows, then on foll 3 [4: 1: 2: 5] alt rows. 55 [59: 65: 69: 73] sts.

Work 1 row, ending after chart row 52 and with RS facing for next row.

Now using yarn A **only**, complete front as folls:

Dec 1 st at each end of next and foll 7 [8: 9: 10: 11] alt rows. 39 [41: 45: 47: 49] sts.

Work 1 row, ending with RS facing for next row.

Shape front neck

Next row (RS): K2, K2tog, K3 [3: 5: 5: 5] and turn, leaving rem sts on a holder. 6 [6: 8: 8: 8] sts.

Work each side of neck separately.

Working any raglan armhole decreases as set, cont as folls:

3-4 and 5-6 years only

Dec 1 st at neck edge of next row. 5 sts.

Next row (RS): K2, K3tog.

Next row: P2tog, P1. 2 sts.

7-8, 9-10 and 11-12 years only

Dec 1 st at neck edge of next 3 rows and at same time dec 1 st at raglan armhole edge of 2nd row. 4 sts.

Next row (RS): K1, sl 1, K2tog, psso.

Next row: P2.

All sizes

Next row: K2tog and fasten off.

Return to sts left on holder and slip centre 25 [27: 27: 29: 31] sts onto another holder (for neckband). Rejoin yarn with RS facing and K to last 4 sts, K2tog tbl, K2. 6 [6: 8: 8: 8] sts. Complete to match first side, reversing shapings.

SLEEVES

Using 3¼mm (US 3) needles and yarn B cast on 30 [30: 30: 34: 34] sts.

Work in rib as given for back for 2 rows, ending with RS facing for next row.

Break off yarn B and join in yarn A.

Cont in rib until sleeve meas 6 [6: 6: 7: 7] cm, dec [inc: inc: dec: dec] 1 st at centre of last row and ending with RS facing for next row. 29 [31: 31: 33: 33] sts.

Change to 4mm (US 6) needles.

Beg with a K row, now work in st st throughout as folls:

Inc 1 st at each end of 3rd [5th: 3rd: 3rd: 3rd] and every foll 6th [6th: 4th: 4th: 6th] row to 45 [47: 37: 37: 63] sts, then on every foll – [8th: 6th: 6th: –] row until there are – [49: 55: 59: –] sts.

Cont straight until sleeve meas 24 [28: 32: 36: 41] cm, ending with RS facing for next row.

Shape raglan

Cast off 3 sts at beg of next 2 rows. 39 [43: 49: 53: 57] sts.

Working all raglan decreases in same way as raglan armhole decreases, dec 1 st at each end of next and 3 foll 4th rows, then on every foll alt row until 17 sts rem.

Work 1 row, ending with RS facing for next row.

Left sleeve only

Dec 1 st at each end of next row, then cast off 3 sts at beg of foll row. 12 sts.

Dec 1 st at beg of next row, then cast off 4 sts at beg of foll row. 7 sts.

Dec 1 st at beg of next row, then cast off 3 sts at beg of foll row.

Right sleeve only

Cast off 4 sts at beg and dec 1 st at end of next row. 12 sts.

Work 1 row.

Rep last 2 rows once more. 7 sts.

Cast off 3 sts at beg and dec 1 st at end of next row.

Work 1 row.

Both sleeves

Cast off rem 3 sts.

MAKING UP

Press as described on the information page.

Join all raglan seams.

Neckband

With RS facing, using double-pointed 3¼mm (US 3) needles and yarn A, pick up and knit 12 sts from top of left sleeve, and 4 [4: 6: 6: 6] sts down left side of front neck, K across 25 [27: 27: 29: 31] sts on front holder inc 1 [1: 0: 0: 0] st at centre, pick up and knit 4 [4: 6: 6: 6] sts up right side of front neck, and 12 sts from top of right sleeve, then K across 29 [31: 33: 35: 37] sts on back holder inc 1 [1: 0: 0: 0] st at centre. 88 [92: 96: 100: 104] sts.

Distribute sts evenly over 3 of the 4 needles and, using 4th needle, work in rounds as folls:

Round 1 (RS): ★K2, P2, rep from ★ to end.

This round forms rib.

Work in rib for a further 4 [4: 4: 6: 6] rounds.

Cast off **loosely** in rib. (**Note**: Make sure cast-off edge will stretch sufficiently to easily fit over child's head!)

See information page for finishing instructions.

Join side and sleeve seams.

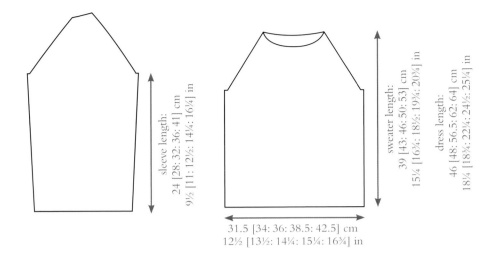

sleeve length:
24 [28: 32: 36: 41] cm
9½ [11: 12½: 14¼: 16¼] in

sweater length:
39 [43: 46: 50: 53] cm
15¼ [16¾: 18½: 19¾: 20¾] in

dress length:
46 [48: 56.5: 62: 64] cm
18¼ [18¾: 22¼: 24½: 25¼] in

31.5 [34: 36: 38.5: 42.5] cm
12½ [13½: 14¼: 15¼: 16¾] in

Bark Chart

Key

☐ Yarn A
⊡ Yarn B

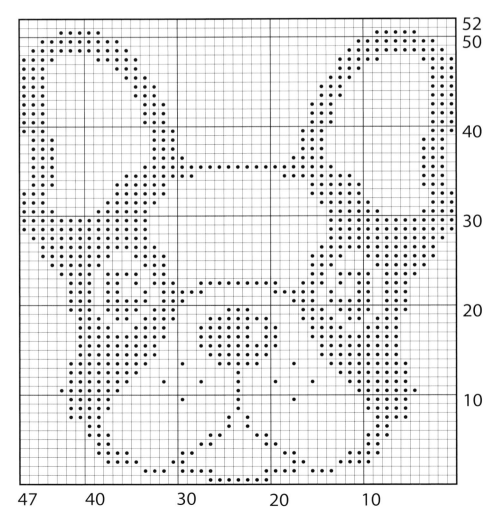

Mini Alexie

by Martin Storey

● ● ●

image page 16

SIZE

To fit age

| 3-4 | 5-6 | 7-8 | 9-10 | 11-12 | years |

To fit chest

| 53-56 | 59-61 | 64-66 | 69-74 | 76-79 | cm |
| 21-22 | 23-24 | 25-26 | 27-29 | 30-31 | in |

Actual chest measurement of garment

| 87.5 | 95.5 | 100.5 | 108.5 | 118 | cm |
| 34½ | 37½ | 39½ | 42¾ | 46½ | in |

YARN

Softyak DK

| 11 | 11 | 12 | 13 | 13 | x 50gm |

(photographed in Submarine 251)

NEEDLES

1 pair 3¼mm (no 10) (US 3) needles
1 pair 4mm (no 8) (US 6) needles
Cable needle

TENSION

30 sts and 32 rows to 10 cm measured over patt using 4mm (US 6) needles. Cable panel (67 sts) measures 20 cm.

SPECIAL ABBREVIATIONS

C4B = slip next 2 sts onto cable needle and leave at back of work, K2, then K2 from cable needle; **C4F** = slip next 2 sts onto cable needle and leave at front of work, K2, then K2 from cable needle; **C4L** = slip next 3 sts onto cable needle and leave at front of work, K1, then K3 from cable needle; **C4R** = slip next st onto cable needle and leave at back of work, K3, then K1 from cable needle; **C7B** = slip next 4 sts onto cable needle and leave at back of work, K3, then K4 from cable needle; **C7F** = slip next 3 sts onto cable needle and leave at front of work, K4, then K3 from cable needle; **Cr3L** = slip next 2 sts onto cable needle and leave at front of work, P1, then K2 from cable needle; **Cr3R** = slip next st onto cable needle and leave at back of work, K2, then P1 from cable needle; **Cr4L** = slip next 3 sts onto cable needle and leave at front of work, P1, then K3 from cable needle; **Cr4R** = slip next st onto cable needle and leave at back of work, K3, then P1 from cable needle.

BACK

Using 3¼mm (US 3) needles cast on 131 [143: 151: 163: 177] sts.
Row 1 (RS): P0 [1: 1: 0: 0], K1 [2: 2: 1: 0], ★P2, K2, rep from ★ to last 2 [0: 0: 2: 1] sts, P2 [0: 0: 2: 1].
Row 2: K0 [1: 1: 0: 0], P1 [2: 2: 1: 0], ★K2, P2, rep from ★ to last 2 [0: 0: 2: 1] sts, K2 [0: 0: 2: 1].
These 2 rows form patt.
Work in patt for a further 6 rows, ending with RS facing for next row.
Change to 4mm (US 6) needles.
Cont in patt until back meas 50 [53: 58: 63: 67] cm, ending with RS facing for next row.
Shape shoulders and back neck
Cast off 8 [8: 9: 10: 11] sts at beg of next 2 rows, then 8 [9: 9: 10: 11] sts at beg of foll 4 rows. 83 [91: 97: 103: 111] sts.
Next row (RS): Cast off 8 [9: 9: 10: 11] sts, patt until there are 19 [21: 23: 24: 26] sts on right needle and turn, leaving rem sts on a holder.
Work each side of neck separately.
Dec 1 st at neck edge of next 3 rows, ending with RS facing for next row, **and at same time** cast off 8 [9: 10: 10: 11] sts at beg of 2nd row.
Cast off rem 8 [9: 10: 11: 12] sts.
Return to sts left on holder and rejoin yarn with RS facing.
Cast off centre 29 [31: 33: 35: 37] sts then patt to end.
Complete to match first side, reversing shapings.

POCKET LININGS (make 2)

Using 4mm (US 6) needles cast on 25 sts.
Beg with a K row, work in st st for 39 rows, ending with **WS** facing for next row.
Row 40 (WS): P5, (M1P, P3) 5 times, M1P, P5.
Break yarn and leave 31 sts on a holder.

LEFT FRONT

Using 3¼mm (US 3) needles cast on 76 [81: 84: 89: 95] sts.

Row 1 (RS): K0 [2: 2: 0: 1], ★P2, K2, rep from ★ to last 8 [7: 10: 9: 10] sts, P1 [0: 2: 2: 2], K0 [0: 1: 0: 1], (P1, K1 tbl) 3 times, K1.

Row 2: (K1, P1) 3 times, K1 [0: 1: 1: 1], P0 [0: 2: 1: 2], ★K2, P2, rep from ★ to last 1 [3: 3: 1: 2] sts, K1 [2: 2: 1: 2], P0 [1: 1: 0: 0].

These 2 rows form patt.

Work in patt for a further 6 rows, ending with RS facing for next row.

Change to 4mm (US 6) needles.

Now place cable panel as folls:

Next row (RS): Patt 9 [14: 17: 22: 28] sts, work rem 67 sts as row 1 of chart for left front.

Next row: Work first 67 sts as row 2 of chart for left front, patt 9 [14: 17: 22: 28] sts.

These 2 rows set the sts – side edge 9 [14: 17: 22: 28] sts in patt as given for back and rem 67 sts in cable patt from chart.

Cont as set for a further 38 rows, ending with RS facing for next row.

Place pocket

Next Row(RS): Patt 10 [15: 18: 23: 29] sts, slip next 31 sts onto a holder and, in their place, patt across 31 sts of first pocket lining, patt rem 35 sts.

Cont straight until left front matches back to beg of shoulder shaping, ending with RS facing for next row.

Shape shoulder

Keeping patt correct, cast off 8 [9: 10: 10: 11] sts at beg of next and foll 1 [2: 5: 0: 0] alt rows, then 9 [10: –: 11: 12] sts at beg of foll 4 [3: –: 5: 5] alt rows. 24 sts.

Inc 1 st at end of next row. 25 sts.

Cont in patt on these 25 sts only (for back neck border extension) until this strip meas 6 [6.5: 6.5: 7: 7.5] cm, ending with RS facing for next row.

Cast off in patt.

RIGHT FRONT

Using 3¼mm (US 3) needles cast on 76 [81: 84: 89: 95] sts.

Row 1 (RS): K1, (K1 tbl, P1) 3 times, P0 [1: 0: 0: 0], K0 [2: 2: 1: 2], ★P2, K2, rep from ★ to last 1 [3: 3: 1: 2] sts, P1 [2: 2: 1: 2], K0 [1: 1: 0: 0].

Row 2: P0 [2: 2: 0: 1], ★K2, P2, rep from ★ to last 8 [7: 10: 9: 10] sts, K1 [0: 2: 2: 2], P0 [0: 1: 0: 1], (K1, P1) 3 times, K1.

These 2 rows form patt.

Work in patt for a further 6 rows, ending with RS facing for next row.

Change to 4mm (US 6) needles.

Now place cable panel as folls:

Next row (RS): Work first 67 sts as row 1 of chart for right front, patt 9 [14: 17: 22: 28] sts.

Next row: Patt 9 [14: 17: 22: 28] sts, work rem 67 sts as row 2 of chart for right front.

These 2 rows set the sts – side edge 9 [14: 17: 22: 28] sts in patt as given for back and rem 67 sts in cable patt from chart.

Cont as set for a further 38 rows, ending with RS facing for next row.

Place pocket

Next row (RS): Patt 35 sts, slip next 31 sts onto a holder and, in their place, patt across 31 sts of second pocket lining, patt rem 10 [15: 18: 23: 29] sts.

Complete to match left front, reversing shapings.

SLEEVES

Using 3¼mm (US 3) needles cast on 75 [79: 83: 87: 91] sts.

Row 1 (RS): K1, P2, ★K2, P2, rep from ★ to end.

Row 2: P1, K2, ★P2, K2, rep from ★ to end.

These 2 rows form patt.

Work in patt for a further 6 rows, ending with RS facing for next row.

Cont in patt, shaping sides by inc 1 st at each end of next and every foll 30th [16th: 10th: 6th: 6th] row to 81 [83: 99: 93: 105] sts, then on every foll – [18th: 12th: 8th: 8th] row until there are – [89: 101: 113: 123] sts, taking inc sts into patt.

Cont straight until sleeve meas 24 [28: 32: 36: 41] cm, ending with RS facing for next row.

Cast off in patt.

MAKING UP

Press as described on the information page.

Join both shoulder seams, easing in cable section on fronts.

Join cast-off ends of back neck border extensions, then sew one edge to back neck edge.

Pocket tops (both alike)

Slip 31 sts from pocket holder onto 3¼mm (US 3) needles and rejoin yarn with RS facing.

Row 1 (RS): K1, P2, (K1, K2tog, P2) twice, K2, P2, (K2, P1, P2tog) twice, K2, P2. 27 sts.

Beg with row 2, work in patt as given for sleeves for 3 rows, ending with RS facing for next row.

Cast off in patt.

Belt

Using 3¼mm (US 3) needles cast on 11 sts.

Row 1 (RS): K1, (K1 tbl, P1) 4 times, K1 tbl, K1.

Row 2: K1, (P1, K1) 5 times.

These 2 rows form rib.

Cont in rib until belt meas 110 [120: 125: 135: 150] cm, ending with RS facing for next row.

Cast off in rib.

Mark points along side seam edges 14.5 [16: 18: 20: 21.5] cm either side of shoulder seams (to denote base of armhole openings). See information page for finishing instructions, setting in sleeves using the straight cast-off method.

Join side and sleeve seams. Slip stitch pocket edgings and linings into place.

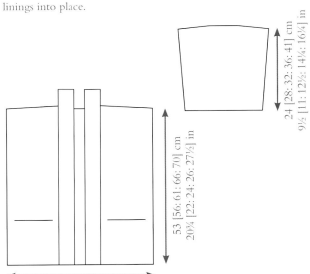

24 [28: 32: 36: 41] cm
9½ [11: 12½: 14¼: 16¼] in

53 [56: 61: 66: 70] cm
20¾ [22: 24: 26: 27½] in

43.5 [47.5: 50.5: 54.5: 59] cm
17¼ [18¾: 19¾: 21½: 23¼] in

Right Front Alexie Chart

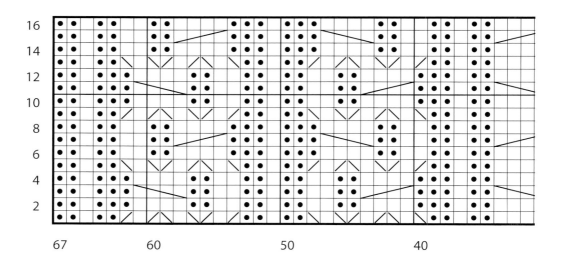

Left Front Alexie Chart

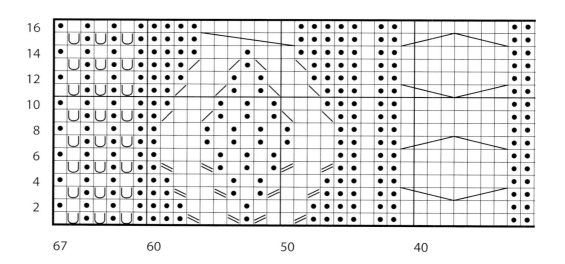

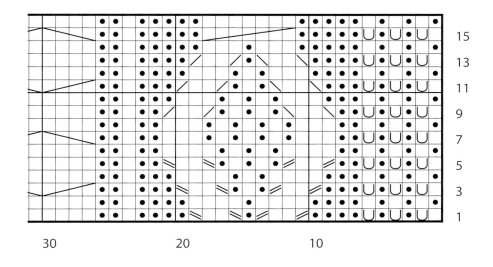

15
13
11
9
7
5
3
1

30   20   10

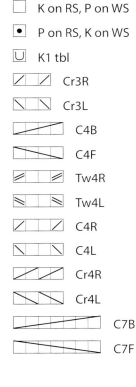

Key

☐ K on RS, P on WS

● P on RS, K on WS

U K1 tbl

⟋⟋ Cr3R

⟍⟍ Cr3L

C4B

C4F

Tw4R

Tw4L

C4R

C4L

Cr4R

Cr4L

C7B

C7F

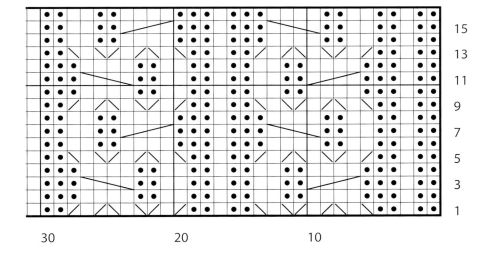

15
13
11
9
7
5
3
1

30   20   10

Mini Ellen

by Kaffe Fassett

● ● ●

image page 18

SIZE

To fit age

| 3-4 | 5-6 | 7-8 | 9-10 | 11-12 | years |

To fit chest

| 53-56 | 59-61 | 64-66 | 69-74 | 76-79 | cm |
| 21-22 | 23-24 | 25-26 | 27-29 | 30-31 | in |

Actual chest measurement of garment

| 62.5 | 68.5 | 71.5 | 77.5 | 84 | cm |
| 24½ | 27 | 28¼ | 30½ | 33 | in |

YARN

Cotton Glace

A Dawn Grey 831					
2	2	3	3	4	50gm
B Persimmon 832					
1	1	1	2	2	50gm
C Cobalt 850					
1	1	1	2	2	50gm
D Shell 845					
1	1	1	2	2	50gm
E Shoot 814					
1	1	2	2	2	50gm
F Mineral 856					
1	1	2	2	2	50gm
G Heather 828					
1	1	2	2	2	50gm
H Aqua 858					
1	1	2	2	2	50gm
I Oyster 730					
1	1	1	2	2	50gm

NEEDLES

1 pair 3¼mm (no 10) (US 3) needles

TENSION

26 sts and 29 rows to 10 cm measured over patterned st st using 3¼mm (US 3) needles.

Chart note: Chart is a repeat of an **ODD** number of rows. On first and third rep of chart, odd numbered rows are RS (K) rows, and on second rep of chart odd numbered rows are **WS** (P) rows.

BACK

Using 3¼mm (US 3) needles and yarn A cast on 82 [90: 94: 102: 110] sts.

Row 1 (RS): K2, ★P2, K2, rep from ★ to end.
Row 2: P2, ★K2, P2, rep from ★ to end.
These 2 rows form rib.

Cont in rib for a further 4 [4: 6: 6: 6] rows, dec 1 st at end of last row and ending with RS facing for next row. 81 [89: 93: 101: 109] sts.

Beg and ending rows as indicated, using the **fairisle** technique as described on the information page, repeating the 8-st patt repeat 10 [11: 11: 12: 13] times across each row and repeating the 63-row patt repeat throughout (see chart note), cont in patt from chart, which is worked entirely in st st beg with a K row, as folls:

Cont straight until back meas 24.5 [27: 30: 32: 33.5] cm, ending with RS facing for next row.

Shape armholes

Keeping patt correct, cast off 5 [6: 6: 6: 7] sts at beg of next 2 rows. 71 [77: 81: 89: 95] sts.

Dec 1 st at each end of next 5 [5: 5: 7: 7] rows, then on foll 4 [6: 6: 5: 6] alt rows. 53 [55: 59: 65: 69] sts.★★

Work 21 [21: 25: 31: 33] rows, ending with RS facing for next row. (Armhole should meas 12.5 [14: 15: 17: 18.5] cm.)

Shape shoulders and back neck

Keeping patt correct, cont as folls:

Next row (RS): Cast off 5 [5: 5: 6: 7] sts, patt until there are 8 [8: 9: 10: 10] sts on right needle and turn, leaving rem sts on a holder.

Work each side of neck separately.

Cast off 3 sts at beg of next row.

Cast off rem 5 [5: 6: 7: 7] sts.

Return to sts left on holder and slip centre 27 [29: 31: 33: 35] sts onto another holder (for neckband). Rejoin appropriate yarns with RS facing and patt to end. Complete to match first side, reversing shapings.

FRONT

Work as given for back to ★★.
Work 1 [1: 3: 9: 9] rows, ending with RS facing for next row.
Shape front neck
Next row (RS): Patt 19 [19: 21: 23: 25] sts and turn, leaving rem sts on a holder.
Work each side of neck separately.
Keeping patt correct, dec 1 st at neck edge of next 4 rows, then on foll 4 [4: 5: 5: 6] alt rows, then on foll 4th row. 10 [10: 11: 13: 14] sts.
Work 3 rows, ending with RS facing for next row.
Shape shoulder
Cast off 5 [5: 5: 6: 7] sts at beg of next row.
Work 1 row.
Cast off rem 5 [5: 6: 7: 7] sts.
Return to sts left on holder and slip centre 15 [17: 17: 19: 19] sts onto another holder (for neckband). Rejoin appropriate yarns with RS facing and patt to end. Complete to match first side, reversing shapings.

MAKING UP

Press as described on the information page.
Join right shoulder seam.
Neckband
With RS facing, using 3¼mm (US 3) needles and yarn A, pick up and knit 22 [22: 24: 24: 26] sts down left side of front neck, K across 15 [17: 17: 19: 19] sts on front holder inc 1 [1: 0: 0: 1] st at centre, pick up and knit 22 [22: 24: 24: 26] sts up right side of front neck, and 3 sts down right side of back neck, K across 27 [29: 31: 33: 35] sts on back holder inc 1 [1: 0: 0: 1] st at centre, then pick up and knit 3 sts up left side of back neck. 94 [98: 102: 106: 114] sts.
Beg with row 2, work in rib as given for back for 4 [4: 6: 6: 6] rows, ending with **WS** facing for next row.
Cast off **loosely** in rib (on **WS**) using a bigger needle if required. (**Note:** Make sure cast-off edge will stretch sufficiently to easily fit over child's head!)
Join left shoulder and neckband seam.
Armhole borders (both alike)
With RS facing, using 3¼mm (US 3) needles and yarn A, pick up and knit 78 [86: 94: 102: 110] sts evenly along armhole edge.
Beg with row 2, work in rib as given for back for 4 [4: 6: 6: 6] rows, ending with **WS** facing for next row.
Cast off in rib (on **WS**).
Join side seam and armhole border seams.
See information page for finishing instructions.

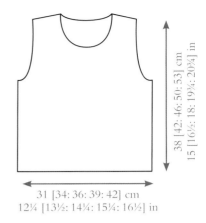

38 [42: 46: 50: 53] cm
15 [16½: 18: 19¾: 20¾] in

31 [34: 36: 39: 42] cm
12¼ [13½: 14¼: 15¼: 16½] in

Ellen Chart

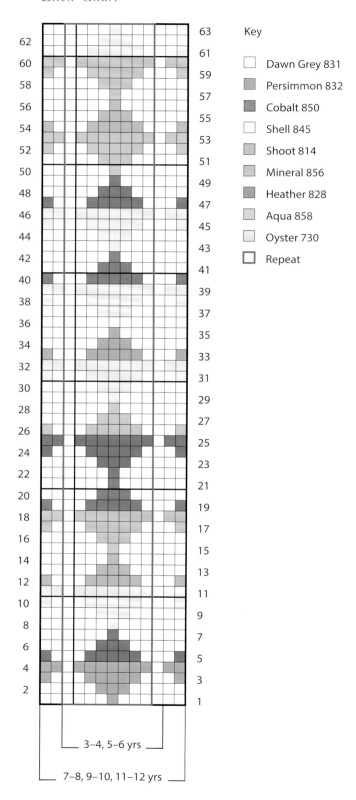

Key

- ☐ Dawn Grey 831
- ▨ Persimmon 832
- ▨ Cobalt 850
- ☐ Shell 845
- ▨ Shoot 814
- ▨ Mineral 856
- ▨ Heather 828
- ▨ Aqua 858
- ▨ Oyster 730
- ☐ Repeat

3–4, 5–6 yrs

7–8, 9–10, 11–12 yrs

Mini Cornwallis

by Martin Storey

● ●

image page 20

———————

SIZE

To fit age

| 3–4 | 5–6 | 7–8 | 9–10 | 11–12 | years |

To fit chest

| 53–56 | 59–61 | 64–66 | 69–74 | 76–79 | cm |
| 21–22 | 23–24 | 25–26 | 27–29 | 30–31 | in |

Actual chest measurement of garment

| 62.5 | 68 | 72 | 77.5 | 84.5 | cm |
| 24½ | 26¾ | 28¼ | 30½ | 33¼ | in |

YARN

Summerlite DK

A White 465

| 2 | 3 | 3 | 3 | 3 | x 50gm |

B Sailor Blue 470

| 2 | 2 | 2 | 3 | 3 | x 50gm |

C Summer 453

| 1 | 2 | 2 | 2 | 2 | x 50gm |

NEEDLES

1 pair 3¼mm (no 10) (US 3) needles
1 pair 3¾mm (no 9) (US 5) needles

TENSION

22 sts and 30 rows to 10 cm measured over st st, 21 sts and 40 rows to 10 cm measured over g st, both using 3¾mm (US 5) needles.

BACK

Using 3¼mm (US 3) needles and yarn A cast on 69 [75: 79: 85: 93] sts.

Beg with a K row, work in st st throughout as folls:

Work 4 rows, ending with RS facing for next row.

Change to 3¾mm (US 5) needles.

Work a further 4 rows, ending with RS facing for next row.

Now work in st st in stripes as folls:

Join in yarn B.

Using yarn B, work 4 rows.

Using yarn A, work 4 rows.

Last 8 rows form striped st st.

Cont in striped st st until back meas approx 26.5 [29.5: 32: 34.5: 34.5] cm, ending after 4 rows using yarn A and with RS facing for next row.

Shape raglan armholes

Keeping stripes correct, cast off 3 sts at beg of next 2 rows. 63 [69: 73: 79: 87] sts.

Dec 1 st at each end of next and foll 4th row, ending after 3 rows using yarn A and with **WS** facing for next row. 59 [65: 69: 75: 83] sts.

Next row (WS): Using yarn A, P6 [6: 8: 8: 9], P2tog, (P13 [15: 15: 17: 19], P2tog) 3 times, P6 [6: 8: 8: 9]. 55 [61: 65: 71: 79] sts.

Break off yarns A and B and join in yarn C.

Now complete back in g st using yarn C **only** as folls:

Dec 1 st at each end of 3rd and 5 [6: 8: 9: 9] foll 4th rows, then on foll 7 [8: 7: 8: 11] alt rows. 29 [31: 33: 35: 37] sts.

Work 1 row, ending with RS facing for next row.

Break yarn and leave sts on a holder.

FRONT

Work as given for back until 43 [47: 49: 51: 55] sts rem in raglan armhole shaping.

Work 1 [1: 3: 1: 1] rows, ending with RS facing for next row.

Shape front neck

Next row (RS): K2tog, K9 [11: 11: 11: 13] and turn, leaving rem sts on a holder. 10 [12: 12: 12: 14] sts.

Work each side of neck separately.

Dec 1 st at neck edge of next 4 rows, then on foll 1 [2: 2: 2: 3] alt rows **and at same time** dec 1 st at raglan armhole edge of 2nd and foll 2 [3: 3: 3: 4] alt rows. 2 sts.

Work 1 row.

Next row (RS): K2tog and fasten off.

Return to sts left on holder and slip centre 21 [21: 23: 25: 25] sts onto another holder (for neckband). Rejoin yarn with RS facing and K decreasing 1 st at end of row to match back. Complete to match first side, reversing shapings.

SLEEVES

Using 3¼mm (US 3) needles and yarn A cast on 37 [39: 41: 43: 43] sts.

Beg with a K row, work in st st throughout as folls:

Work 4 rows, ending with RS facing for next row.

Change to 3¾mm (US 5) needles.

Work a further 4 rows, ending with RS facing for next row. Join in yarn B.

Now working in striped st st as given for back, beg with 4 rows using yarn B, cont as folls:

Inc 1 st at each end of next and every foll 8th [8th: 6th: 6th: 6th] row to 43 [51: 47: 49: 61] sts, then on every foll 10th [10th: 8th: 8th: 8th] row until there are 51 [57: 63: 69: 75] sts.

Cont straight until sleeve meas approx. 24 [29.5: 32: 37.5: 42.5] cm, ending after 4 rows using yarn A and with RS facing for next row.

Shape raglan

Keeping stripes correct, cast off 3 sts at beg of next 2 rows. 45 [51: 57: 63: 69] sts.

Dec 1 st at each end of next and foll 4th row, ending after 3 rows using yarn A and with **WS** facing for next row. 41 [47: 53: 59: 65] sts.

Next row (WS): Using yarn A, P9 [11: 12: 6: 6], P2tog, (P19 [21: 25: 13: 15], P2tog) 1 [1: 1: 3: 3] times, P9 [11: 12: 6: 6]. 39 [45: 51: 55: 61] sts.

Break off yarns A and B and join in yarn C.

Now complete sleeve in g st using yarn C **only** as folls:

Dec 1 st at each end of 3rd and 2 [2: 2: 3: 3] foll 4th rows, then on foll 10 [13: 16: 17: 20] alt rows. 13 sts.

Work 1 row, ending with RS facing for next row.

Left sleeve only

Dec 1 st at each end of next row, then cast off 3 sts at beg (front neck edge) of foll row. 8 sts.

Dec 1 st at front neck edge of next 4 rows **and at same time** dec 1 st at back raglan edge of next and foll alt row. 2 sts.

Right sleeve only

Cast off 3 sts at beg (front neck edge) and dec 1 st at end of next row. 9 sts.

Dec 1 st at front neck edge of next 5 rows **and at same time** dec 1 st at back raglan edge of 2nd and foll alt row.

Both sleeves

Next row (RS): K2tog and fasten off.

MAKING UP

Press as described on the information page.

Join right front, left front and right back raglan seams.

Neckband

With RS facing, using 3¼mm (US 3) needles and yarn C, pick up and knit 7 sts from top of left sleeve, and 7 [9: 9: 9: 11] sts down left side of front neck, K across 21 [21: 23: 25: 25] sts on front holder, pick up and knit 7 [9: 9: 9: 11] sts up right side of front neck, and 7 sts from top of right sleeve, then K across 29 [31: 33: 35: 37] sts on back holder. 78 [84: 88: 92: 98] sts.

Beg with a **purl** row, work in st st for 4 [4: 6: 6: 6] rows, ending with **WS** facing for next row.

Cast off **loosely** purlwise (on **WS**). (**Note**: Make sure cast-off edge will stretch sufficiently to easily fit over child's head!) Join left back raglan and neckband seam. Join side and sleeve seams.

See information page for finishing instructions.

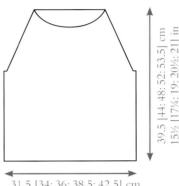

31.5 [34: 36: 38.5: 42.5] cm
12½ [13½: 14¼: 15¼: 16¾] in

39.5 [44: 48: 52: 53.5] cm
15½ [17¼: 19: 20½: 21] in

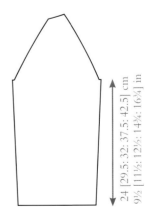

24 [29.5: 32: 37.5: 42.5] cm
9½ [11½: 12½: 14¾: 16¾] in

Mini Hank

by Martin Storey

● ● ●

image page 22

SIZE

To fit age

| 3-4 | 5-6 | 7-8 | 9-10 | 11-12 | years |

To fit chest

| 53-56 | 59-61 | 64-66 | 69-74 | 76-79 | cm |
| 21-22 | 23-24 | 25-26 | 27-29 | 30-31 | in |

Actual chest measurement of garment (measured over g st section)

| 64.5 | 70 | 75.5 | 81 | 86.5 | cm |
| 25½ | 27½ | 29¾ | 32 | 34 | in |

YARN

Softyak DK

| 5 | 6 | 6 | 7 | 7 | x 50gm |

(photographed in Canopy 254 & Shell 247)

NEEDLES

1 pair 3¼mm (no 10) (US 3) needles
1 pair 4mm (no 8) (US 6) needles
Cable needle

TENSION

22 sts and 40 rows to 10 cm measured over g st, 29 sts and 36 rows to 10 cm measured over cable patt, both using 4mm (US 6) needles.

SPECIAL ABBREVIATIONS

C4B = slip next st onto cable needle and leave at back of work, K3, then K1 from cable needle; **C4F** = slip next 3 sts onto cable needle and leave at front of work, K1, then K3 from cable needle; **C6B** = slip next 3 sts onto cable needle and leave at back of work, K3, then K3 from cable needle; **Cr4L** = slip next 3 sts onto cable needle and leave at front of work, P1, then K3 from cable needle; **Cr4R** = slip next st onto cable needle and leave at back of work, K3, then P1 from cable needle.

BACK

Using 3¼mm (US 3) needles cast on 90 [98: 102: 114: 122] sts.
Row 1 (RS): K2, ★P2, K2, rep from ★ to end.
Row 2: P2, ★K2, P2, rep from ★ to end.
These 2 rows form rib.
Cont in rib for a further 14 [14: 16: 16: 16] rows, inc 1 [0: 1: 1: 0] st at each end of last row and ending with RS facing for next row. 92 [98: 104: 116: 122] sts.
Change to 4mm (US 6) needles.
Beg and ending rows as indicated, repeating the 26-st patt repeat 3 [3: 3: 4: 4] times across each row and repeating the 28-row patt repeat throughout, cont in patt from appropriate chart for body for size being knitted as folls:
Cont in patt until all 28 rows of chart for body have been completed 3 [3: 3: 4: 4] times in total, and then work chart rows 1 to 3 again, ending with **WS** facing for next row.
Next row (WS): K4 [7: 10: 3: 6], (P2tog) 3 times, ★K7, (P2tog) 3 times, rep from ★ to last 4 [7: 10: 3: 6] sts, K4 [7: 10: 3: 6]. 71 [77: 83: 89: 95] sts.
Now working in g st throughout, complete back as folls:
Cont straight until back meas 37.5 [41.5: 45.5: 49.5: 52.5] cm, ending with RS facing for next row.
Shape shoulders and back neck
Cast off 2 [3: 3: 3: 3] sts at beg of next 4 [8: 8: 8: 4] rows, then 3 [-: -: -: 4] sts at beg of foll 4 [-: -: -: 4] rows. 51 [53: 59: 65: 67] sts.
Next row (RS): Cast off 3 [3: 3: 4: 4] sts, K until there are 14 [14: 16: 17: 17] sts on right needle and turn, leaving rem sts on a holder.
Work each side of neck separately.
Dec 1 st at neck edge of next 5 rows, ending with RS facing for next row, **and at same time** cast off 3 [3: 3: 4: 4] sts at beg of 2nd row, then 3 [3: 4: 4: 4] sts at beg of foll alt row.
Cast off rem 3 [3: 4: 4: 4] sts.
Return to sts left on holder and slip centre 17 [19: 21: 23: 25] sts onto another holder (for neckband). Rejoin yarn with RS facing and K to end. Complete to match first side, reversing shapings.

FRONT

Work as given for back until 4 [6: 6: 6: 10] rows less have been worked than on back to beg of shoulder shaping, ending with RS facing for next row.

Shape front neck

Next row (RS): K29 [32: 34: 36: 39] and turn, leaving rem sts on a holder.

Work each side of neck separately.

Dec 1 st at neck edge of next 3 [4: 4: 4: 4] rows, then on foll 0 [0: 0: 0: 2] alt rows. 26 [28: 30: 32: 33] sts.

Work 0 [1: 1: 1: 1] row, ending with RS facing for next row.

Shape shoulder

Cast off 2 [3: 3: 3: 3] sts at beg of next and foll 1 [6: 5: 3: 1] alt rows, then 3 [-: 4: 4: 4] sts at beg of foll 5 [-: 1: 3: 5] alt rows **and at same time** dec 1 st at neck edge of next and foll 2 [2: 2: 2: 0] alt rows, then on 1 [1: 1: 1: 2] foll 4th rows.

Work 1 row.

Cast off rem 3 [3: 4: 4: 4] sts.

Return to sts left on holder and slip centre 13 [13: 15: 17: 17] sts onto another holder (for neckband). Rejoin yarn with RS facing and K to end. Complete to match first side, reversing shapings.

SLEEVES

Using 3¼mm (US 3) needles cast on 38 [38: 42: 42: 46] sts.

Work in rib as given for back for 16 [16: 18: 18: 18] rows, inc 0 [1: 0: 1: 0] st at each end of last row and ending with RS facing for next row. 38 [40: 42: 44: 46] sts.

Change to 4mm (US 6) needles.

Beg and ending rows as indicated and repeating the 28-row patt repeat throughout, cont in patt from chart for sleeve as folls:

Inc 1 st at each end of 5th [3rd: 3rd: 3rd: 3rd] and foll 0 [0: 1: 1: 1] alt row, then on every foll 4th row until there are 64 [76: 84: 92: 102] sts, then on 1 [0: 0: 0: 0] foll 6th row, taking inc sts into patt. 66 [76: 84: 92: 102] sts. (**Note:** Sleeve shaping is only shown on chart for first 28-row patt repeat.)

Cont straight until sleeve meas 24 [28: 32: 36: 41] cm, ending with RS facing for next row.

Cast off in patt.

MAKING UP

Press as described on the information page.

Join right shoulder seam.

Neckband

With RS facing and using 3¼mm (US 3) needles, pick up and knit 14 [17: 17: 17: 18] sts down left side of front neck, K across 13 [13: 15: 17: 17] sts on front holder, pick up and knit 14 [17: 17: 17: 18] sts up right side of front neck, and 4 sts down right side of back neck, K across 17 [19: 21: 23: 25] sts on back holder, then pick up and knit 4 sts up left side of back neck. 66 [74: 78: 82: 86] sts.

Beg with row 2, work in rib as given for back for 5 [5: 7: 7: 7] rows, ending with RS facing for next row.

Cast off **loosely** in rib on a larger needle. (**Note**: Make sure cast-off edge will stretch sufficiently to easily fit over child's head!)

Join left shoulder and neckband seam.

Mark points along side seam edges 12.5 [14: 15.5: 17: 18.5] cm either side of shoulder seams (to denote base of armhole openings). See information page for finishing instructions, setting in sleeves using the straight cast-off method.

Join side and sleeve seams.

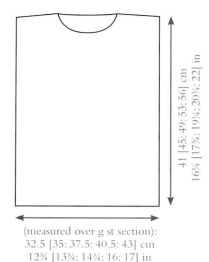

(measured over g st section):
32.5 [35: 37.5: 40.5: 43] cm
12¾ [13¾: 14¾: 16: 17] in

41 [45: 49: 53: 56] cm
16¼ [17¾: 19¼: 20¾: 22] in

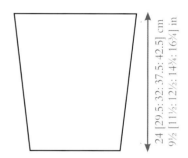

24 [29.5: 32: 37.5: 42.5] cm
9½ [11½: 12½: 14¾: 16¾] in

Hank Body Charts

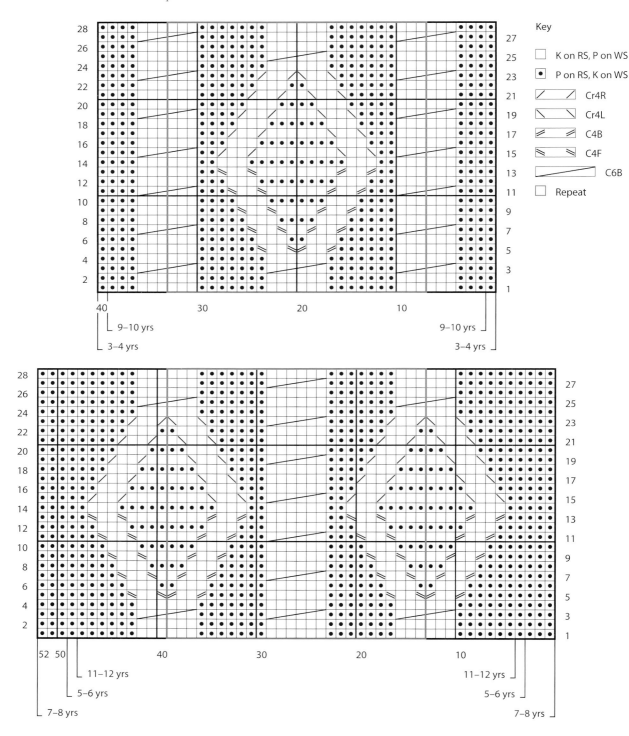

Key

☐ K on RS, P on WS

• P on RS, K on WS

╱ ╱ Cr4R

╲ ╲ Cr4L

▨ ▨ C4B

▨ ▨ C4F

⬚ C6B

☐ Repeat

Hank Sleeve Chart

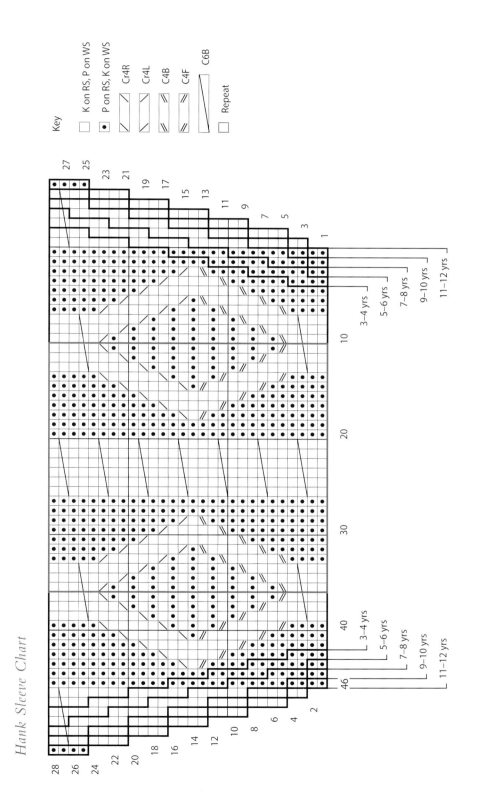

Key

☐ K on RS, P on WS

● P on RS, K on WS

Cr4R

Cr4L

C4B

C4F

C6B

☐ Repeat

B

Mini Barton

by Martin Storey

● ●

image page 24

―――――――

SIZE

To fit age

| 3–4 | 5–6 | 7–8 | 9–10 | 11–12 | years |

To fit chest

| 53–56 | 59–61 | 64–66 | 69–74 | 76–79 | cm |
| 21–22 | 23–24 | 25–26 | 27–29 | 30–31 | in |

Actual chest measurement of garment

| 62.5 | 68 | 73.5 | 81 | 86.5 | cm |
| 24½ | 26¾ | 29 | 32 | 34 | in |

YARN

Denim Revive

A Night 213 / Night 213

| 5 | 5 | 5 | 6 | 6 | x 50gm |

B Lipstick 214 / Blue Wash 211

| 3 | 3 | 4 | 4 | 4 | x 50gm |

NEEDLES

1 pair 3¼mm (no 10) (US 3) needles
1 pair 3¾mm (no 9) (US 5) needles
2 double-pointed 3¼mm (no 10) (US 3) needles
1 spare 3¾mm (no 9) (US 5) needle for bind-off

EXTRAS

Stitch holders
Stitch marker

BUTTONS – 5

TENSION

22 sts and 29 rows to 10 cm measured over st st using 3¾mm (US 5) needles.

BACK

Using 3¼mm (US 3) needles and yarn A, cast on 70 [74: 82: 90: 94] sts.

Row 1 (RS): K2, ★P2, K2, rep from ★ to end.

Row 2: P2, ★K2, P2, rep from ★ to end.

These 2 rows form rib.

Cont in rib until back meas 4 [4: 5: 5: 5] cm, dec [inc: dec: dec: inc] 1 st at end of last row and ending with RS facing for next row. 69 [75: 81: 89: 95] sts.

Change to 3¾mm (US 5) needles.

Beg with a K row, now work in st st as folls:

Using yarn A, work 2 rows.

Join in yarn B.

Using yarn B, work 2 rows.

Last 4 rows form striped st st.

Keeping striped st st correct throughout, cont as folls:

Cont straight until back meas 28.5 [31: 33.5: 36: 37.5] cm, ending with RS facing for next row.

Shape armholes

Keeping stripes correct, cast off 3 [3: 3: 4: 4] sts at beg of next 2 rows. 63 [69: 75: 81: 87] sts.

Dec 1 st at each end of next 3 [3: 5: 5: 5] rows, then on foll 2 [4: 3: 4: 4] alt rows. 53 [55: 59: 63: 69] sts.

Cont straight until armhole meas 12 [13.5: 15: 16.5: 18] cm, ending with RS facing for next row.

Shape shoulders and back neck

Keeping stripes correct, cast off 4 [4: 5: 5: 6] sts at beg of next 2 rows. 45 [47: 49: 53: 57] sts.

Next row (RS): Cast off 4 [4: 5: 5: 6] sts, K until there are 8 [8: 7: 8: 8] sts on right needle and turn, leaving rem sts on a holder.

Work each side of neck separately.

Cast off 3 sts at beg of next row.

Cast off rem 5 [5: 4: 5: 5] sts.

Return to sts left on holder, rejoin appropriate yarn with RS facing, cast off 21 [23: 25: 27: 29] sts, then K to end. Complete to match first side, reversing shapings.

POCKET LININGS (make 2)

Using 3¾mm (US 5) needles and yarn A, cast on 23 [25: 25: 27: 27] sts.

Beg with a K row and 2 rows using yarn A, work in striped st st as given for back for 4 [4: 6: 6: 6] rows, ending with RS facing for next row.

Break yarns and leave sts on a holder.

LEFT FRONT

Using 3¼mm (US 3) needles and yarn A cast on 35 [39: 39: 43: 47] sts.

Row 1 (RS): K2, ★P2, K2, rep from ★ to last st, K1.
Row 2: K1, P2, ★K2, P2, rep from ★ to end.
These 2 rows form rib.

Cont in rib until left front meas 4 [4: 5: 5: 5] cm, dec [dec: inc: inc: -] 1 [2: 1: 1: -] sts evenly across last row and ending with RS facing for next row. 34 [37: 40: 44: 47] sts.

Change to 3¾mm (US 5) needles.

Beg with a K row and 2 rows using yarn A, work in striped st st as given for back as folls:

Work 4 [4: 6: 6: 6] rows, ending with RS facing for next row.

Place pocket

Next row (RS): K7 [8: 11: 13: 16], slip rem 27 [29: 29: 31: 31] sts onto a holder (for pocket front and opening edge) and, in their place, K across 23 [25: 25: 27: 27] sts of first pocket lining.

Cont in striped st st on these 30 [33: 36: 40: 43] sts for a further 29 [33: 37: 37: 41] rows (for pocket lining and side front), ending with RS facing for next row.

Break yarns and leave these sts on another holder.

Return to 27 [29: 29: 31: 31] sts on first holder and rejoin appropriate yarn with RS facing.

Cont in striped st st for 30 [34: 38: 38: 42] rows, ending with RS facing for next row.

Break yarns and return sts to holder.

Join sections

Rejoin appropriate yarn to pocket lining and side front sts with RS facing and cont as folls:

Next row (RS): K first 7 [8: 11: 13: 16] sts, place WS of pocket front against RS of pocket lining, K tog first st of pocket front with next st of pocket lining, (K tog next st of pocket front with next st of pocket lining) 22 [24: 24: 26: 26] times, K rem 4 sts. 34 [37: 40: 44: 47] sts.

Cont straight until left front matches back to beg of armhole shaping, ending with RS facing for next row.

Shape armhole

Keeping stripes correct, cast off 3 [3: 3: 4: 4] sts at beg of next row. 31 [34: 37: 40: 43] sts.

Work 1 row.

Dec 1 st at armhole edge of next 3 [3: 5: 5: 5] rows, then on foll 2 [4: 3: 4: 4] alt rows. 26 [27: 29: 31: 34] sts.

Cont straight until 7 [9: 9: 9: 11] rows less have been worked than on back to shoulder shaping, ending with **WS** facing for next row.

Shape front neck

Keeping stripes correct, cast off 7 [7: 8: 9: 9] sts at beg of next row. 19 [20: 21: 22: 25] sts.

Dec 1 st at neck edge of next 5 rows, then on foll 0 [1: 1: 1: 2] alt rows. 14 [14: 15: 16: 18] sts.

Work 1 row, ending with RS facing for next row.

Shape shoulder

Keeping stripes correct, cast off 4 [4: 5: 5: 6] sts at beg of next and foll alt row **and at same time** dec 1 st at neck edge of next row.

Work 1 row.
Cast off rem 5 [5: 4: 5: 5] sts.

RIGHT FRONT

Using 3¼mm (US 3) needles and yarn A cast on 35 [39: 39: 43: 47] sts.

Row 1 (RS): K3, ★P2, K2, rep from ★ to end.
Row 2: P2, ★K2, P2, rep from ★ to last st, K1.
These 2 rows form rib.

Cont in rib until right front meas 4 [4: 5: 5: 5] cm, dec [dec: inc: inc: -] 1 [2: 1: 1: -] sts evenly across last row and ending with RS facing for next row. 34 [37: 40: 44: 47] sts.

Change to 3¾mm (US 5) needles.

Beg with a K row and 2 rows using yarn A, now work in striped st st as given for back as folls:

Work 4 [4: 6: 6: 6] rows, ending with RS facing for next row.

Place pocket

Next row (RS): K27 [29: 29: 31: 31] and turn, leaving rem 7 [8: 11: 13: 16] sts onto a holder (for side front).

Cont in striped st st on these 27 [29: 29: 31: 31] sts for a further 29 [33: 37: 37: 41] rows (for pocket front and opening edge), ending with RS facing for next row.

Break yarns and leave these sts on another holder.

Return to 7 [8: 11: 13: 16] sts left on first holder and sts of second pocket lining. Rejoin appropriate yarn with RS facing, K across 23 [25: 25: 27: 27] sts of pocket lining, then K side front sts. 30 [33: 36: 40: 43] sts.

Work 29 [33: 37: 37: 41] more rows, ending with RS facing for next row.

Break yarns and leave sts on another holder.

Join sections

Rejoin appropriate yarn to pocket front and opening edge sts with RS facing and cont as folls:

Next row (RS): K first 4 sts, place WS of pocket front against RS of pocket lining, K tog next st of pocket front with first st of pocket lining, (K tog next st of pocket front with next st of pocket lining) 22 [24: 24: 26: 26] times, K rem 7 [8: 11: 13: 16] sts. 34 [37: 40: 44: 47] sts.

Cont right front to match left front, up to Shape front neck, reversing shapings.

Shape front neck

Next row (WS): P19 [20: 21: 22: 25], cast off rem 7 [7: 8: 9: 9] sts.

Break yarn.

Rejoin appropriate yarns with RS facing and complete right front to match left front, reversing shapings.

SLEEVES

Using 3¼mm (US 3) needles and yarn A cast on 30 [30: 30: 34: 34] sts.

Work in rib as given for back for 4 [4: 5: 5: 5] cm, dec [inc: inc: dec: dec] 1 st at end of last row and ending with RS facing for next row. 29 [31: 31: 33: 33] sts.

Change to 3¾mm (US 5) needles.

Beg with a K row and 2 rows using yarn A, cont in striped st st as given for back as folls:

Inc 1 st at each end of 3rd [5th: 3rd: 3rd: 3rd] and every foll 6th [6th: 4th: 4th: 4th] row to 47 [49: 39: 43: 47] sts, then on every foll – [8th: 6th: 6th: 6th] row until there are – [51: 57: 63: 69] sts.

Cont straight until sleeve meas approx 24 [28: 32: 36: 41] cm, ending after same stripe row as on back to beg of armhole shaping and with RS facing for next row.

Shape top

Keeping stripes correct, cast off 3 [3: 3: 4: 4] sts at beg of next 2 rows. 41 [45: 51: 55: 61] sts.

Dec 1 st at each end of next 3 rows, then on foll 7 [10: 11: 14: 15] alt rows, then on foll 5 [3: 5: 3: 5] rows, ending with RS facing for next row.

Cast off rem 11 [13: 13: 15: 15] sts.

HOOD

Using 3¾mm (US 5) needles and yarn A cast on 67 [69: 73: 77: 83] sts.

Beg with a K row and 2 rows using yarn A, work in striped st st as given for back as folls:

Row 1 (RS): K33 [34: 36: 38: 41], place marker for centre st, K to end.

Row 2: P to end.

Row 3: K to 1 st before marker, M1, K3, M1, K to end.

Row 4: P to end.

Row 5: K2, K2tog tbl, yfwd (to make eyelet), K to 1 st before marker, M1, K3, M1, K to last 4 sts, yfwd, K2tog (to make eyelet), K2.

Working all centre back increases as set in row 3, inc 1 st at each side of centre back st on 2nd and 2 foll 4th rows, then on foll 6th row. 79 [81: 85: 89: 95] sts.

Cont straight until hood meas 18 [19: 20: 21: 22] cm, ending with RS facing for next row.

Next row (RS): K to 2 sts before marker, K2tog, K1, sl 1, K1, psso, K to end.

Working all centre back decreases as set by last row, dec 1 st at each side of marked st on 4th and 5 foll alt rows, ending with **WS** facing for next row. 65 [67: 71: 75: 81] sts.

Next row (WS): P to 3 sts before marker, P2tog tbl, P1, P2tog, P to end.

Working all decreases as now set, dec 1 st at each side of centre back st on next 3 rows, ending with **WS** facing for next row. 57 [59: 63: 67: 73] sts.

Next row (WS): P to 2 sts before marker, P2tog, remove marker, turn. 56 [58: 62: 66: 72] sts.

Fold hood in half with RS together and, using spare needle, cast off both sets of 28 [29: 31: 33: 36] sts together (to form top seam of hood).

MAKING UP

Press as described on the information page.

Join both shoulder seams.

Button band

With RS facing, using 3¼mm (US 3) needles and yarn A, pick up and knit 92 [100: 112: 120: 128] sts evenly along one front opening edge (left front for a girl, or right front for a boy) between neck shaping and cast-on edge.

Row 1 (WS): K1, P2, *K2, P2, rep from * to last st, K1.

Row 2: K3, *P2, K2, rep from * to last st, K1.

These 2 rows form rib.

Work in rib for a further 5 rows, ending with RS facing for next row.

Cast off in rib.

Buttonhole band

With RS facing, using 3¼mm (US 3) needles and yarn A, pick up and knit 92 [100: 112: 120: 128] sts evenly along other front opening edge.

Work in rib as given for button band for 3 rows, ending with RS facing for next row.

Next Row (RS): Rib 3, *work 2 tog, yrn (to make a buttonhole), rib 19 [21: 24: 26: 28], rep from * 3 times more, work 2 tog, yrn (to make 5th buttonhole), rib 3.

Work in rib for a further 3 rows, ending with RS facing for next row.

Cast off in rib.

Pocket borders (both alike)

With RS facing, using 3¼mm (US 3) needles and yarn A, pick up and knit 24 [28: 32: 32: 36] sts evenly along row-end edge of pocket opening.

Work in rib as given for button band for 5 rows, ending with RS facing for next row.

Cast off in rib.

Sew pocket linings in place on inside, then neatly sew down ends of pocket borders.

Hood facing

With RS facing, using 3¼mm (US 3) needles and yarn A, pick up and knit 120 [124: 128: 132: 136] sts evenly along entire front opening edge of hood, between cast-on edges.

Work in rib as given for button band for 7 rows, ending with RS facing for next row.

Cast off in rib.

Fold hood facing to inside along pick-up row and neatly sew in place. Positioning fold line of facing midway across top of front bands and easing in slight fullness, sew cast-on edge of hood to neck edge.

Hood drawstring

Using double-pointed 3¼mm (US 3) needles and preferred yarn, cast on 3 sts.

Row 1 (RS): K3, *without turning slip these 3 sts to opposite end of needle and bring yarn to opposite end of work pulling it quite tightly across **WS** of work, K these 3 sts again, rep from * until drawstring is 80 [85: 85: 90: 90] cm long.

Cast off.

Thread drawstring through front hood facing via eyelet holes and secure mid-point at top of hood. Attach buttons. See information page for finishing instructions, setting in sleeves using the set-in method. Join side and sleeve seams.

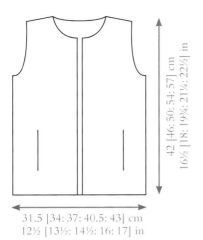

42 [46: 50: 54: 57] cm
16½ [18: 19¾: 21¼: 22½] in

31.5 [34: 37: 40.5: 43] cm
12½ [13½: 14½: 16: 17] in

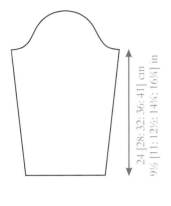

24 [28: 32: 36: 41] cm
9½ [11: 12½: 14¼: 16¼] in

A

Mini Citron

by Quail Studio

image page 26

—————

SIZE
To fit age

3-6   7-9   10-12   years

FINISHED SIZE
Completed hat meas 40 [43: 46] cm (15¾ [17: 18] in) all round head.

YARN
Big Wool

1   1   1   x 100gm

(photographed in Oasis 092, Pumpkin 090, Aurora Pink 084)

NEEDLES
1 pair 10mm (no 000) (US 15) needles

TENSION
10 sts and 12 rows to 10 cm measured over st st using 10mm (US 15) needles.

HAT

Using 10mm (US 15) needles cast on 40 [43: 46] sts.

Row 1 (RS): P1, *K2, P1, rep from * to end.

Row 2: K1, *P2, K1, rep from * to end.

These 2 rows form rib.

Cont in rib until hat meas 5 [7: 8] cm, ending with RS facing for next row.

Beg with a K row, work in st st throughout as folls:

Cont straight until hat meas 16.5 [18.5: 20] cm from cast-on edge, ending with RS facing for next row.

Shape crown

Row 1 (RS): K1, *K2tog, K1, rep from * to end. 27 [29: 31] sts.

Row 2: Purl.

Row 3: K0 [0: 1], *K2tog, K1, rep from * to last 0 [2: 0] sts, (K2tog) 0 [1: 0] time. 18 [19: 21] sts.

Row 4: Purl.

Row 5: K0 [1: 1], (K2tog) 9 [9: 10] times.

Break yarn and thread through rem 9 [10: 11] sts. Pull up tight and fasten off securely.

MAKING UP

Press as described on the information page.

Join back seam, reversing seam for rib turn-back.

See information page for finishing instructions.

Mini Pumpkin

by Quail Studio

image page 26

_____

SIZE
To fit age
3-6   7-9   10-12   years

FINISHED SIZE
Completed snood is 15 [18: 21] cm wide and 70 [80: 90] cm in circumference

YARN
Big Wool
1   1   1   x 100gm
(photographed in Oasis 092, Pumpkin 090, Aurora Pink 084)

NEEDLES
1 pair 10mm (no 000) (US 15) needles
10mm (no 000) (US 15) circular needle

EXTRAS – Oddment of waste yarn (for cast-on)

TENSION
10 sts and 16 rows to 10 cm meas over patt using 10mm (US 15) needles.

SNOOD
Using 10mm (US 15) needles and waste yarn cast on 14 [17: 20] sts.
Row 1 (WS): Purl.
Row 2: Knit.
Break off waste yarn and join in main yarn.
Next row (WS): Purl.
Now work in patt as folls:
Row 1 (RS): P2, ★K1, P2, rep from ★ to end.
Row 2: Purl.
Row 3: Knit.
Row 4: K2, ★P1, K2, rep from ★ to end.
Row 5: Knit.
Row 6: Purl.
These 6 rows form patt.
Cont in patt until work meas approx 70 [80: 90] cm, ending after patt row 5 and with WS facing for next row.
Break yarn leaving a length long enough to sew up seam.

MAKING UP
Press as described on the information page.
Using long end, carefully graft tog sts of first row in main yarn to sts of last row worked to join ends to form a loop, unravelling waste yarn.
Edgings (both like)
With RS facing and using 10mm (US 15) circular needle, beg and ending at grafted seam, pick up and knit 90 [100: 110] sts evenly all round one row-end edge of snood.
Cast off knitwise.
Work edging along other row-end edge in same way.
See information page for finishing instructions.

Mini Bret

by Martin Storey

● ●

image page 28

SIZE
To fit age

3-4	5-6	7-8	9-10	11-12	years

To fit chest

53-56	59-61	64-66	69-74	76-79	cm
21-22	23-24	25-26	27-29	30-31	in

Actual chest measurement of garment

61	66.5	72	77.5	82.5	cm
24	26¼	28¼	30½	32½	in

YARN
Denim Revive

A Night 213

2	3	3	3	4	x 50gm

B Bluewash 211

2	2	3	3	3	x 50gm

NEEDLES
1 pair 3¼mm (no 10) (US 3) needles
1 pair 3¾mm (no 9) (US 5) needles
Set of 4 double-pointed 3¼mm (no 10) (US 3) needles

TENSION
22 sts and 29 rows to 10 cm measured over st st using 3¾mm (US 5) needles.

BACK
Using 3¼mm (US 3) needles and yarn A, cast on 62 [66: 74: 78: 86] sts.
Row 1 (RS): K2, ★P2, K2, rep from ★ to end.
Row 2: P2, ★K2, P2, rep from ★ to end.
These 2 rows form rib.
Cont in rib until back meas 4 [4: 5: 5: 5] cm, dec [inc: dec: inc: dec] 1 st at end of last row and ending with RS facing for next row. 61 [67: 73: 79: 85] sts.
Change to 3¾mm (US 5) needles.
Beg with a K row, now work in striped st st throughout as folls:
Using yarn A, work 2 rows.
Join in yarn B.
Using yarn B, work 2 rows.
Last 4 rows form striped st st.
Cont in striped st st, shaping side seams by inc 1 st at each end of 11th and 2 foll 16th [16th: 18th: 18th: 20th] rows. 67 [73: 79: 85: 91] sts.
Cont straight until back meas 26 [28.5: 31: 33.5: 35] cm, ending with RS facing for next row.
Shape armholes
Keeping stripes correct, cast off 3 [4: 4: 5: 5] sts at beg of next 2 rows. 61 [65: 71: 75: 81] sts.★★
Dec 1 st at each end of next 3 [3: 5: 5: 5] rows, then on foll 4 [5: 4: 4: 5] alt rows. 47 [49: 53: 57: 61] sts.
Cont straight until armhole meas 12 [13.5: 15: 16.5: 18] cm, ending with RS facing for next row.
Shape shoulders and back neck
Keeping stripes correct, cont as folls:
Next row (RS): Cast off 3 [3: 4: 4: 4] sts, K until there are 10 [10: 10: 11: 12] sts on right needle and turn, leaving rem sts on a holder.
Work each side of neck separately.
Dec 1 st at neck edge of next 3 rows, ending with RS facing for next row, **and at same time** cast off 3 [3: 4: 4: 4] sts at beg of 2nd row.

Cast off rem 4 [4: 3: 4: 5] sts.
Return to sts left on holder and slip centre 21 [23: 25: 27: 29] sts onto another holder (for neckband). Rejoin appropriate yarn with RS facing and K to end. Complete to match first side, reversing shapings.

FRONT
Work as given for back to ★★.
Divide for front neck
Keeping stripes correct, cont as folls:
Next row (RS): K2tog, K28 [30: 33: 35: 38] and turn, leaving rem sts on a holder. 29 [31: 34: 36: 39] sts.
Work each side of neck separately.
Dec 1 st at armhole edge of next 2 [2: 4: 4: 4] rows, then on foll 4 [5: 4: 4: 5] alt rows **and at same time** dec 1 st at neck edge of 2nd and foll 4 [5: 5: 5: 6] alt rows. 18 [18: 20: 22: 23] sts.
Dec 1 st at neck edge **only** on 2nd and foll 6 [6: 6: 6: 5] alt rows, then on 1 [1: 2: 3: 4] foll 4th rows. 10 [10: 11: 12: 13] sts.
Cont straight until front matches back to beg of shoulder shaping, ending with RS facing for next row.
Shape shoulder
Keeping stripes correct, cast off 3 [3: 4: 4: 4] sts at beg of next and foll alt row.
Work 1 row.
Cast off rem 4 [4: 3: 4: 5] sts.
Return to sts left on holder and slip centre st onto another holder (for neckband). Rejoin appropriate yarn with RS facing and K to last 2 sts, K2tog. 29 [31: 34: 36: 39] sts.
Complete to match first side, reversing shapings.

MAKING UP
Press as described on the information page.
Join both shoulder seams.
Neckband
With RS facing, using double-pointed 3¼mm (US 3) needles and yarn A, pick up and knit 35 [39: 43: 47: 51] sts down left side of front neck, K st on holder at base of V-neck and mark this st with a coloured thread, pick up and knit 35 [39: 43: 47: 51] sts up right side of front neck, and 3 sts down right side of back neck, K across 21 [23: 25: 27: 29] sts on back holder dec [inc: dec: inc: dec] 1 st at centre, then pick up and knit 3 sts up left side of back neck. 97 [109: 117: 129: 137] sts.
Round 1 (RS): P2, ★K2, P2, rep from ★ 1 st before marked st, K3 (marked st is centre st of these 3 sts), ★★P2, K2, rep from ★★ to end.
This round sets position of rib.
Keeping rib correct, cont as folls:
Round 2: Rib to 1 st before marked st, slip next 2 sts as though to K2tog (marked st is 2nd of these 2 sts), K1, p2sso, rib to end.
Round 3: Rib to marked st, K marked st, rib to end.
Rep last 2 rounds 1 [1: 2: 2: 2] times more. 93 [105: 111: 123: 131] sts.
Cast off **loosely** in rib, still decreasing either side of marked st as before, taking care cast-off edge will stretch over child's head.
Armhole borders (both alike)
With RS facing, using 3¼mm (US 3) needles and yarn A, pick up and knit 62 [70: 78: 90: 98] sts evenly along armhole edge.
Beg with row 2, work in rib as given for back for 5 [5: 7: 7: 7] rows, ending with RS facing for next row.
Cast off in rib.

Join side and armhole border seams.
See information page for finishing instructions.

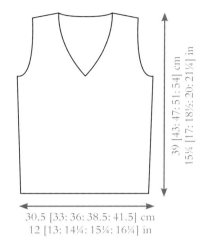

39 [43: 47: 51: 54] cm
15¼ [17: 18½: 20: 21¼] in

30.5 [33: 36: 38.5: 41.5] cm
12 [13: 14¼: 15¼: 16¼] in

Mini Veronica

by Grace Jones

● ●

image page 30

———————

SIZE
To fit age

3-4	5-6	7-8	9-10	11-12	years

To fit chest

53-56	59-61	64-66	69-74	76-79	cm
21-22	23-24	25-26	27-29	30-31	in

Actual chest measurement of garment

73	81	85.5	92	98.5	cm
28¾	32	33¾	36¼	38¾	in

YARN
Summerlite 4 ply

2	3	3	3	4	x 50gm

(photographed in Pure White 417)

NEEDLES
1 pair 3mm (no 11) (US 2/3) needles

TENSION
25 sts and 49 rows to 10 cm measured over g st using 3mm (US 2/3) needles.

SPECIAL ABBREVIATION
sl2togK = slip next 2 sts as though to K2tog.

BACK and FRONT (both alike and knitted downwards, beg at neck and shoulder edges)
Using 3mm (US 2/3) needles cast on 91 [101: 107: 115: 123] sts.
Noting that first row is a RS row, work in g st throughout as folls:
Cont straight until work meas 11 [12.5: 14: 15.5: 17] cm, ending with RS facing for next row.
Place markers at both ends of last row (to denote base of armhole openings).
Shape side seams
Dec 1 st at each end of 19th [11th: 11th: 11th: 9th] and 0 [2: 3: 3: 4] foll 0 [10th: 8th: 8th: 8th] rows. 89 [95: 99: 107: 113] sts.
Work 17 [9: 7: 9: 5] rows, ending with RS facing for next row.
Shape darts
Counting in from both ends of last row, place markers after 22nd [23rd: 24th: 26th: 28th] st in from each end of row – there should be 45 [49: 51: 55: 57] sts between markers at centre of row.
Next row (RS): K to first marker, slip marker onto right needle, sl2togK, K1, p2sso, K to within 3 sts of second marker, sl2togK, K1, p2sso, slip marker onto right needle, K to end.
Work 15 [17: 17: 19: 19] rows.
Rep last 16 [18: 18: 20: 20] rows twice more, then first of these rows (the dec row) again. 73 [79: 83: 91: 97] sts.
Cont straight until work meas 32 [35: 38: 41.5: 43.5] cm **from cast-on edge**, ending with **WS** facing for next row.
Cast off **knitwise** (on **WS**).

MAKING UP
Press as described on the information page.
Mark points along cast-on edges either side of central 20 [21: 22: 23: 24] cm to denote neck opening. Join shoulder seams beyond neck opening points, leaving end 4 [5: 5: 6: 6] cm of seam open (for shoulder openings). Join side seams below markers denoting base of armhole openings.
See information page for finishing instructions.

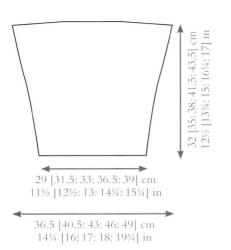

32 [35: 38: 41.5: 43.5] cm
12½ [13¾: 15: 16¼: 17] in

29 [31.5: 33: 36.5: 39] cm
11½ [12½: 13: 14¼: 15¼] in

36.5 [40.5: 43: 46: 49] cm
14¼ [16: 17: 18: 19¼] in

Mini Garrick

by Martin Storey

● ● ●

image page 32

SIZE

To fit age

3-4	5-6	7-8	9-10	11-12	years

To fit chest

53-56	59-61	64-66	69-74	76-79	cm
21-22	23-24	25-26	27-29	30-31	in

Actual chest measurement of garment

63.5	68.5	73.5	78.5	85	cm
25	27	29	31	33½	in

YARN

Denim Revive

A Cream 210

3	4	4	4	5	x 50gm

B Airforce 212

3	3	4	4	5	x 50gm

NEEDLES

1 pair 3¼mm (no 10) (US 3) needles
1 pair 3¾mm (no 9) (US 5) needles

TENSION

24 sts and 24 rows to 10 cm measured over patterned st st using 3¾mm (US 5) needles.

BACK

Using 3¼mm (US 3) needles and yarn A cast on 75 [81: 87: 93: 101] sts.
★★Join in yarn B.
Stranding yarn not in use across WS of work (this is back of work on RS rows, and front of work on WS rows), cont in 2-colour rib as folls:
Row 1 (RS): Using yarn A K1, ★using yarn B P1, using yarn A K1, rep from ★ to end.
Row 2: Using yarn A P1, ★using yarn B K1, using yarn A P1, rep from ★ to end.
These 2 rows form 2 colour rib.**★★**
Cont in rib until back meas 4 [4: 5: 5: 5] cm, inc 1 st at end of last row and ending with RS facing for next row. 76 [82: 88: 94: 102] sts.
Change to 3¾mm (US 5) needles.
Beg and ending rows as indicated, using the **fairisle** technique as described on the information page, beg with chart row 1 and repeating the 76-row patt repeat throughout, cont in patt from chart, which is worked entirely in st st beg with a K row, as folls:
Cont straight until back meas 39 [43: 47: 51: 54] cm, ending with RS facing for next row.
Shape shoulders and back neck
Keeping patt correct, cast off 8 [8: 9: 10: 11] sts at beg of next 2 rows. 60 [66: 70: 74: 80] sts.
Next row (RS): Cast off 8 [8: 9: 10: 11] sts, patt until there are 10 [12: 12: 12: 13] sts on right needle and turn, leaving rem sts on a holder.
Work each side of neck separately.
Cast off 3 sts at beg of next row.
Cast off rem 7 [9: 9: 9: 10] sts.
Return to sts left on holder and slip centre 24 [26: 28: 30: 32] sts onto another holder (for neckband). Rejoin yarns with RS facing and patt to end. Complete to match first side, reversing shapings.

FRONT

Work as given for back until 8 [8: 8: 10: 10] rows less have been worked than on back to beg of shoulder shaping, ending with RS facing for next row.

Shape front neck

Next row (RS): Patt 29 [31: 33: 36: 39] sts and turn, leaving rem sts on a holder.

Work each side of neck separately.

Dec 1 st at neck edge of next 4 rows, then on foll 1 [1: 1: 2: 2] alt rows. 24 [26: 28: 30: 33] sts.

Work 1 row, ending with RS facing for next row.

Shape shoulder

Keeping patt correct, cast off 8 [8: 9: 10: 11] sts at beg of next and foll alt row **and at same time** dec 1 st at neck edge of next row.

Work 1 row.

Cast off rem 7 [9: 9: 9: 10] sts.

Return to sts left on holder and slip centre 18 [20: 22: 22: 24] sts onto another holder (for neckband). Rejoin yarns with RS facing and patt to end. Complete to match first side, reversing shapings.

SLEEVES

Using 3¼mm (US 3) needles and yarn A cast on 31 [33: 35: 37: 37] sts.

Work as given for back from ★★ to ★★.

Cont in rib until sleeve meas 4 [4: 5: 5: 5] cm, inc 1 st at end of last row and ending with RS facing for next row. 32 [34: 36: 38: 38] sts.

Change to 3¾mm (US 5) needles.

Beg and ending rows as indicated, cont in patt from chart as folls:

Inc 1 st at each end of 3rd and foll 0 [2: 3: 5: 5] alt rows, then on every foll 4th row until there are 54 [62: 68: 76: 82] sts, taking inc sts into patt. (**Note:** Sleeve shaping is only shown on chart for first 30 rows.)

Cont straight until sleeve meas 30 [32.5: 34: 36.5: 41] cm, ending with RS facing for next row.

Cast off.

MAKING UP

Press as described on the information page.

Join right shoulder seam.

Neckband

With RS facing, using 3¼mm (US 3) needles and yarn A, pick up and knit 11 [11: 11: 13: 13] sts down left side of front neck, K across 18 [20: 22: 22: 24] sts on front holder, pick up and knit 11 [11: 11: 13: 13] sts up right side of front neck, and 3 sts down right side of back neck, K across 24 [26: 28: 30: 32] sts on back holder inc 1 st at centre, then pick up and knit 3 sts up left side of back neck. 71 [75: 79: 85: 89] sts.

Join in yarn B.

Beg with row 2, work in 2-colour rib for 5 [5: 7: 7: 7] rows, ending with RS facing for next row.

Using yarn A, cast off **loosely** in rib on bigger needle. (**Note:** Make sure cast-off edge will stretch sufficiently to easily fit over child's head!)

Join left shoulder and neckband seam. Mark points along side seam edges 12 [13.5: 15: 16.5: 18] cm either side of shoulder seams (to denote base of armhole openings).

See information page for finishing instructions, setting in sleeves using the straight cast-off method.

Join side and sleeve seams.

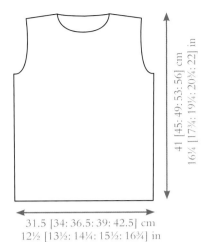

41 [45: 49: 53: 56] cm
16¼ [17¾: 19¼: 20¾: 22] in

31.5 [34: 36.5: 39: 42.5] cm
12½ [13½: 14¼: 15½: 16¾] in

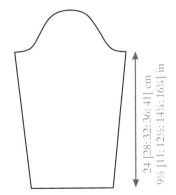

24 [28: 32: 36: 41] cm
9½ [11: 12½: 14¼: 16¼] in

Garrick Body Chart

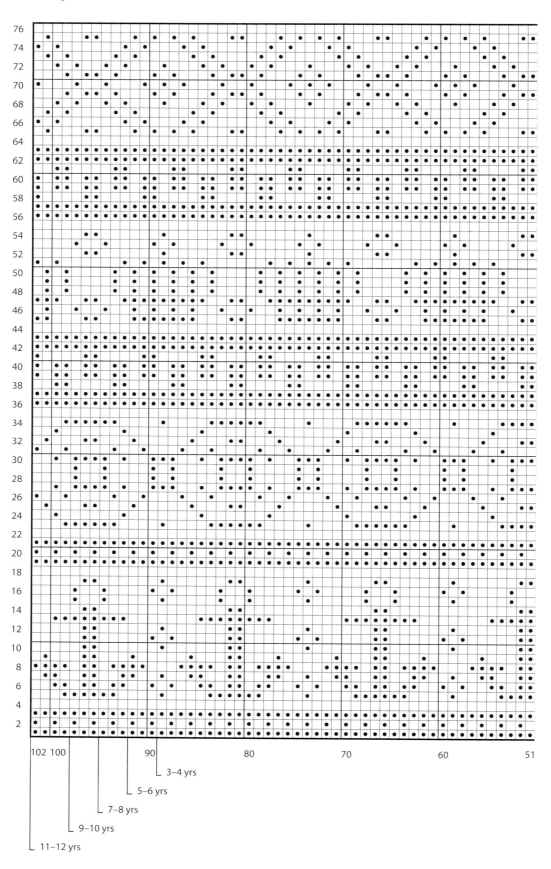

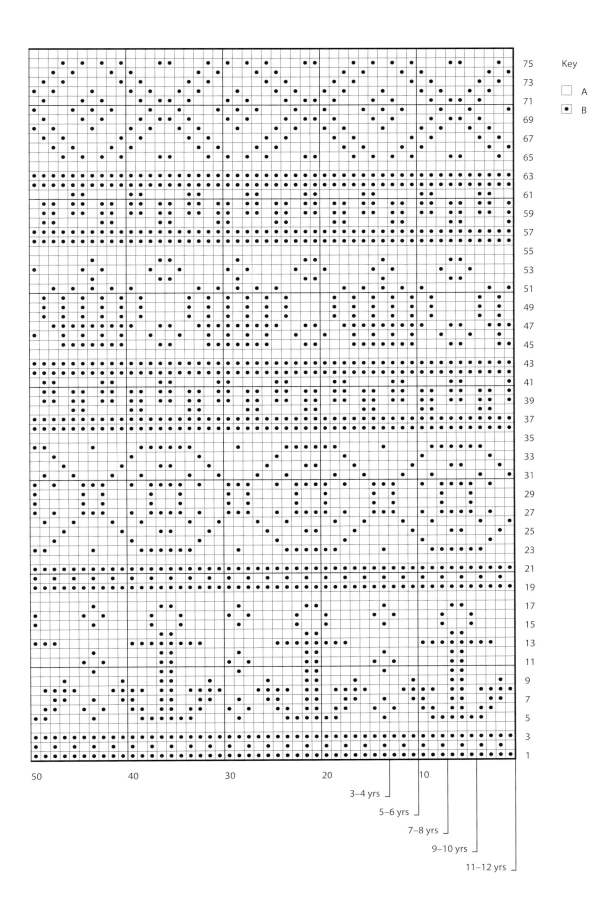

Key

A

• B

75
73
71
69
67
65
63
61
59
57
55
53
51
49
47
45
43
41
39
37
35
33
31
29
27
25
23
21
19
17
15
13
11
9
7
5
3
1

50   40   30   20   10

3–4 yrs ⌐

5–6 yrs ⌐

7–8 yrs ⌐

9–10 yrs ⌐

11–12 yrs ⌐

Garrick Sleeve Chart

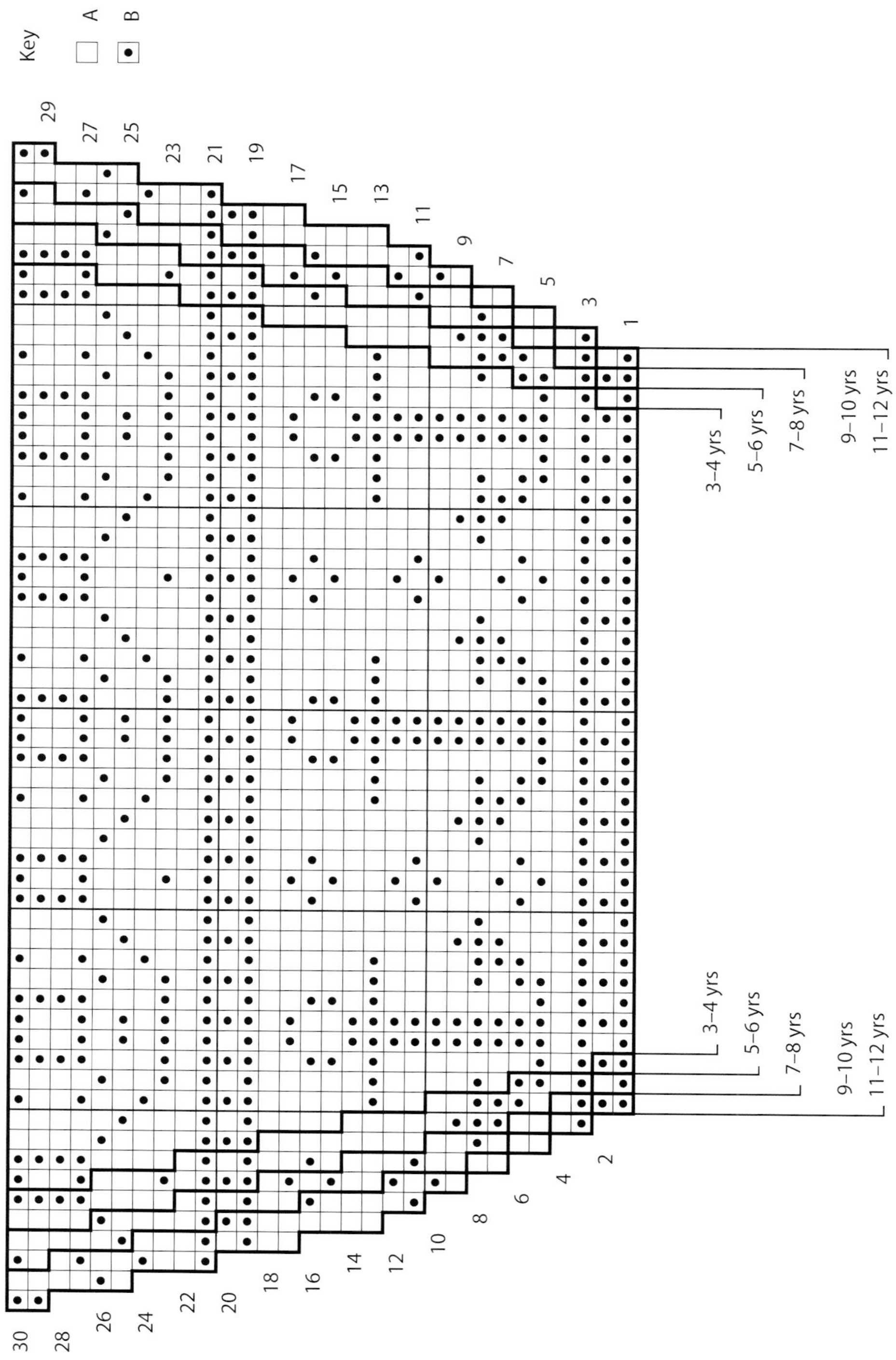

Key

A

B

3–4 yrs
5–6 yrs
7–8 yrs
9–10 yrs
11–12 yrs

3–4 yrs
5–6 yrs
7–8 yrs
9–10 yrs
11–12 yrs

INFORMATION

TENSION

Obtaining the correct tension is perhaps the single factor which can make the difference between a successful garment and a disastrous one. It controls both the shape and size of an article, so any variation, however slight, can distort the finished garment. Different designers feature in our books and it is their tension, given at the start of each pattern, which you must match. We recommend that you knit a square in pattern and/or stocking stitch (depending on the pattern instructions) of perhaps 5 - 10 more stitches and 5 - 10 more rows than those given in the tension note. Mark out the central 10cm square with pins. If you have too many stitches to 10cm try again using thicker needles, if you have too few stitches to 10cm try again using finer needles. Once you have achieved the correct tension your garment will be knitted to the measurements indicated in the size diagram shown at the end of the pattern.

CHART NOTE

Many of the patterns in the book are worked from charts. Each square on a chart represents a stitch and each line of squares a row of knitting. Each colour used is given a different letter and these are shown in the materials section, or in the key alongside the chart of each pattern. When working from the charts, read odd rows (K) from right to left and even rows (P) from left to right, unless otherwise stated. When working lace from a chart it is important to note that all but the largest size may have to alter the first and last few stitches in order not to lose or gain stitches over the row.

WORKING A LACE PATTERN

When working a lace pattern it is important to remember that if you are unable to work both the increase and corresponding decrease and vice versa, the stitches should be worked in stocking stitch.

KNITTING WITH COLOUR

There are two main methods of working colour into a knitted fabric: **Intarsia** and **Fairisle** techniques. The first method produces a single thickness of fabric and is usually used where a colour is only required in a particular area of a row and does not form a repeating pattern across the row, as in the fairisle technique.

Fairisle type knitting: When two or three colours are worked repeatedly across a row, strand the yarn not in use loosely behind the stitches being worked. If you are working with more than two colours, treat the "floating" yarns as if they were one yarn and always spread the stitches to their correct width to keep them elastic. It is advisable not to carry the stranded or "floating" yarns over more than three stitches at a time, but to weave them under and over the colour you are working. The "floating" yarns are therefore caught at the back of the work.

Intarsia: The simplest way to do this is to cut short lengths of yarn for each motif or block of colour used in a row. Then joining in the various colours at the appropriate point on the row, link one colour to the next by twisting them around each other where they meet on the wrong side to avoid gaps. All ends can then either be darned along the colour join lines, as each motif is completed or then can be "knitted-in" to the fabric of the knitting as each colour is worked into the pattern. This is done in much the same way as "weaving- in" yarns when working the Fairisle technique and does save time darning-in ends. It is essential that the tension is noted for intarsia as this may vary from the stocking stitch if both are used in the same pattern.

FINISHING INSTRUCTIONS

After working for hours knitting a garment, it seems a great pity that many garments are spoiled because such little care is taken in the pressing and finishing process. Follow the text below for a truly professional-looking garment.

PRESSING

Block out each piece of knitting and following the instructions on the ball band press the garment pieces, omitting the ribs. Tip: Take special care to press the edges, as this will make sewing up both easier and neater. If the ball band indicates that the fabric is not to be pressed, then covering the blocked out fabric with a damp white cotton cloth and leaving it to stand will have the desired effect. Darn in all ends neatly along the selvedge edge or a colour join, as appropriate.

STITCHING

When stitching the pieces together, remember to match areas of colour and texture very carefully where they meet. Use a seam stitch such as mattress stitch or back stitch for all main knitting seams and join all ribs and neckband with mattress stitch, unless otherwise stated.

CONSTRUCTION

Having completed the pattern instructions, join left shoulder and neckband seams as detailed above. Sew the top of the sleeve to the body of the garment using the method detailed in the pattern, referring to the appropriate guide:

Straight cast-off sleeves: Place centre of cast-off edge of sleeve to shoulder seam. Sew top of sleeve to body, using markers as guidelines where applicable.

Square set-in sleeves: Place centre of cast-off edge of sleeve to shoulder seam. Set sleeve head into armhole, the straight sides at top of sleeve to form a neat right-angle to cast-off sts at armhole on back and front.

Shallow set-in sleeves: Place centre of cast off edge of sleeve to shoulder seam. Match decreases at beg of armhole shaping to decreases at top of sleeve. Sew sleeve head into armhole, easing in shapings.

Set-in sleeves: Place centre of cast-off edge of sleeve to shoulder seam. Set in sleeve, easing sleeve head into armhole.

Join side and sleeve seams.
Slip stitch pocket edgings and linings into place.
Sew on buttons to correspond with buttonholes.
Ribbed welts and neckbands and any areas of garter stitch should not be pressed.
Wash as directed on the ball band.

ABBREVIATIONS

K	knit
P	purl
st(s)	stitch(es)
inc	increas(e)(ing)
dec	decreas(e)(ing)
st st	stocking stitch (1 row K, 1 row P)
g st	garter stitch (K every row)
beg	begin(ning)
foll	following
rem	remain(ing)
rev st st	reverse stocking stitch (1 row K , 1 row P)
rep	repeat
alt	alternate
cont	continue
patt	pattern
tog	together
mm	millimetres
cm	centimetres
in(s)	inch(es)
RS	right side
WS	wrong side
sl 1	slip one stitch
psso	pass slipped stitch over
p2sso	pass 2 slipped stitches over
tbl	through back of loop
M1	make one stitch by picking up horizontal loop before next stitch and knitting into back of it
M1P	make one stitch by picking up horizontal loop before next stitch and purling into back of it
yfwd	yarn forward
yrn	yarn round needle
meas	measures
0	no stitches, times or rows
–	no stitches, times or rows for that size
yon	yarn over needle
yfrn	yarn forward round needle
wyib	with yarn at back
wyif	with yarn at front

CROCHET TERMS

UK crochet terms and abbreviations have been used throughout. The list below gives the US equivalent where they vary.

ABBREVIATIONS

UK	**(US)**
dc (sc)	double crochet (single crochet)
htr (hdc)	half treble (half double crochet)
tr (dc)	treble (double crochet)
dtr (tr)	double treble (treble)

EXPERIENCE RATING
(For guidance only)

⬤ **Beginner Techniques**

For the beginner knitter, basic garment shaping and straight forward stitch technique.

⬤ ⬤ **Simple Techniques**

Simple straight forward knitting, introducing various shaping techniques and garments.

⬤ ⬤ ⬤ **Experienced Techniques**

For the more experienced knitter, using more advanced shaping techniques at the same time as colourwork or different stitch techniques.

⬤ ⬤ ⬤ ⬤ **Advanced Techniques**

Advanced techniques used, using advanced stitches and garment shapings and more challenging techniques

SIZING GUIDE

When you knit a children's design, we want you to be happy with the look and feel of the finished garment. This all starts with the size and fit of the design you choose. To help you to achieve the correct fit for your child, please refer to the sizing chart below. Dimensions in the chart are body measurements, not garment dimensions, therefore please refer to the measuring guide to help you to determine which is the best size for your child.

STANDARD SIZING GUIDE FOR CHILDREN

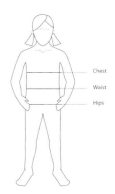

AGE	3 – 4 yrs	5 – 6 yrs	7 – 8 yrs	9 – 10 yrs	11 – 12 yrs	
To fit height	98 – 104	110 – 116	122 – 128	134 – 140	146 – 152	cm
To fit chest	31	34	36	39	42	cm
	12.¼	13½	14¼	15¼	16½	in
To fit waist	30	32	34	36	38	cm
	11¾	13½	13½	14¼	15	in

SIZING & SIZE DIAGRAM NOTE

The instructions are given for the smallest size. Where they vary, work the figures in brackets for the larger sizes. One set of figures refers to all sizes. Included with most patterns in this magazine is a 'size diagram' – see image on the right, of the finished garment and its dimensions. The measurement shown at the bottom of each 'size diagram' shows the garment width 2.5cm below the armhole shaping. To help you choose the size of garment to knit please refer to the sizing guide. Generally in the majority of designs the welt width (at the cast on edge of the garment) is the same width as the chest. However, some designs are 'A-Line' in shape or flared edge and in these cases welt width will be wider than the chest width.

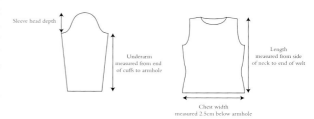

MEASURING GUIDE

For maximum comfort and to ensure the correct fit when choosing the size to knit, please follow the tips below when checking the size of your baby or child.
Measure as close to the body over underwear, but don't pull the tape measure too tight!

Height
measure from the top of your child's head to their feet when they are laying or standing straight.
Chest
measure around the fullest part of the chest and across the shoulder blades.
Waist
measure around the natural waistline just above the hip bone.
Hips
measure around the fullest part of the bottom.

If you don't wish to measure your child's, note the size of their or your favourite jumper that you like the fit of. Our sizes are comparable to the clothing sizes from the major high street retailers, so if the favourite jumper is 6 months or 3 years, then our 6 months or 3 years size should measure approximately the same. Measure this favourite jumper and compare the measurements against the size diagram at the end of the pattern you wish to knit.

Finally, once you have decided which size is best for you to knit, please ensure that you achieve the correct tension for the design you are planning to knit.

Remember if your tension is too loose, your garment will be bigger than the pattern size and you may use more yarn. If your tension is too tight, your garment will be smaller than the pattern size and you may have yarn left over. Furthermore if your tension is incorrect, the handle of your fabric will be either too stiff or too floppy and will not fit properly. As you invest money and time in knitting one of our designs, it really does make sense to check your tension before starting your project.

MODEL INFORMATION
Bianca & Henry wore size 5 – 6 years

Plume
from CAROUSEL

Share your sense of style with cute and cosy matching Rowan fashion...

Skibo
from Mag 68

Hepburn & Tracy
from Mag 67

Bark
from UNION

Alexie
from Mag 69

Ellen
from Mag 67

Cornwallis
from SUMMERLITE DK
COLLECTION

Hank
from UNION

Barton
from OCEAN BLUE

Citron & Pumpkin
from FOUR PROJECTS BIG
WOOL BRIGHTS

Bret
from OCEAN BLUE

Veronica
from Mag 69

Garrick
from UNION

AUSTRALIA: Morris and Sons
Level 1, 234 Collins Street, Melbourne Vic 3000
Tel: 03 9654 0888   **Web**: morrisandsons.com.au

AUSTRALIA: Morris and Sons
50 York Street, Sydney NSW 2000
Tel: 02 92998588   **Web**: morrisandsons.com.au

AUSTRIA: DMC
5 Avenue de Suisse BP 189, Illzach (France)
Email: info-FR@dmc.com

BELGIUM: DMC
5 Avenue de Suisse BP 189, Illzach (France)
Email: info-FR@dmc.com

CANADA: Sirdar USA Inc.
86 Northfield Avenue, Edison , New Jersey, USA 8837
Tel: 1-800-275-4117   **Email**: sirdarusa@sirdar.co.uk
Web: www.sirdar.com

CHINA: Commercial Agent Mr Victor Li,
Email: victor.li@mezcrafts.com

CHINA: Shanghai Yujun CO.LTD.
Room 701 Wangjiao Plaza, No.175 Yan'an Road, 200002 Shanghai, China
Tel: +86 2163739785   **Email**: jessechang@vip.163.com

CZECH REPULIC: Miliimport s.r.o.
Ke Koupalisti 262   Halze, 34701
Tel: + 42 0374783369   **Email**: info@miliimport.cz
Web: www.miliimport.cz

DENMARK: Carl J. Permin A/S
Egegaardsvej 28 DK-2610 Rødovre
Tel: (45) 36 36 89 89   **Email**: permin@permin.dk
Web: www.permin.dk

ESTONIA: Mez Crafts Estonia OÜ
Helgi tee 2, Peetri alevik, Tallinn, 75312 Harjumaa
Tel: +372 6 306 759   **Email**: info.ee@mezcrafts.com
Web: www.mezcrafts.ee

FINLAND: Prym Consumer Finland Oy
Huhtimontie 6, 04200 KERAVA   **Tel**: +358 9 274871
Email: sales.fi@prym.com

FRANCE: DMC
5 Avenue de Suisse BP 189, Illzach (France)
Email: info-FR@dmc.com

GERMANY: DMC
5 Avenue de Suisse BP 189, Illzach (France)
Email: info-DE@dmc.com

HOLLAND: G. Brouwer & Zn B.V.
Oudhuijzenweg 69, 3648 AB Wilnis
Tel: 0031 (0) 297-281 557   **Email**: info@gbrouwer.nl

HONG KONG: CHEER WOOL
Unit C, 9/F, V GA Building, 532 Castle Peak Road, Cheung Shanwan, Kowloon
Tel: 2527-3919   **Email**: info@cheerwool.com
Web: www.cheerwool.com

ICELAND: Carl J. Permin A/S
Egegaardsvej 28, DK-2610 Rødovre
Tel: (45) 36 72 12 00   **Email**: permin@permin.dk   **Web**: www.permin.dk

ITALY: DMC
Via Magenta 77/5, Rho (Milano)   **Email**: info-IT@dmc.com

JAPAN: DMC KK
Santo Building 7F,13, Kanda Konya Cho, Chiyodaku, 101-0035 , Tokyo
Email: ouchi@dmc-kk.com

KOREA: My Knit Studio
3F, 59 Insadong-gil, Jongno-gu, 03145, Seoul
Tel: 82-2-722-0006   **Email**: myknitstudio@myknit.com
Web: www.myknit.com

LEBANON: y.knot
Saifi Village, Mkhalissiya Street 162, Beirut
Tel: (961) 1 992211   **Email**: y.knot@cyberia.net.lb

LITHUANIA: UAB GERAS KRAITIS
Jonavos 68F, Kaunas, Kaunas, LT-44191
Tel: 37067153080   **Email**: info@geraskraitis.lt

LUXEMBOURG: DMC
5 Avenue de Suisse BP 189, Illzach (France)
Email: info-FR@dmc.com

NEW ZEALAND: Trendy Trims
7 Angle Street, Onehunga, Auckland, New Zealand
Email: trendy@trendytrims.co.nz   **Web**: trendytrims.co.nz

NORWAY: Carl J. Permin A/S
Andersrudveien 1, 1914, Ytre Enebakk
Tel: 23 16 35 30   **Email**: permin@permin.dk
Web: www.permin.dk

PORTUGAL: DMC
P. Ferrocarriles Catalanes, 117 oficina 34, Cornellá de llobregat, 08940
Email: info-PT @dmc.com

RUSSIA: Family Hobby
Zelenograd, Haus 1505, Raum III, 124683
Email: tv@fhobby.ru   **Web**: www.family-hobby.ru

SOUTH AFRICA: Arthur Bales LTD
62 4th Avenue, Linden 2195
Tel: (27) 11 888 2401   **Email**: info@arthurbales.co.za
Web: www.arthurbales.co.za

SPAIN: DMC
P. Ferrocarriles Catalanes, 117 oficina 34, Cornellá de llobregat, 08940
Email: info-SP @dmc.com

SWEDEN: Carl J. Permin A/S
Skaraborgsvägen 35C, 3tr, Borås
Tel: 33 12 77 10   **Email**: sverige@permin.dk
Web: www.permin.dk

SWITZERLAND: DMC
5 Avenue de Suisse BP 189, Illzach (France)
Email: info-DE@dmc.com

U.S.A.: Sirdar USA Inc
86 Northfield Avenue, Edison , New Jersey, USA 8837
Tel: 1-800-275-4117   **Email**: sirdarusa@sirdar.co.uk
Web: www.sirdar.com

U.K: Rowan
Flanshaw Lane, Alverthorpe, Wakefield, WF2 9ND, United Kingdom
Tel: 01924 371501   **Email**: mail@knitrowan.com

For more stockists in all countries please log on to
www.knitrowan.com